Atonement at Ground Zero

Atonement at Ground Zero

Revisiting the Epicenter of Salvation

MICHAEL McNICHOLS

RESOURCE *Publications* • Eugene, Oregon

ATONEMENT AT GROUND ZERO
Revisiting the Epicenter of Salvation

Copyright © 2012 Michael McNichols. All rights reserved. Except for brief quotations in critical publications or reviews, no part of this book may be reproduced in any manner without prior written permission from the publisher. Write: Permissions, Wipf and Stock Publishers, 199 W. 8th Ave., Suite 3, Eugene, OR 97401.

Resource Publications
An Imprint of Wipf and Stock Publishers
199 W. 8th Ave., Suite 3
Eugene, OR 97401
www.wipfandstock.com

ISBN 13: 978-1-61097-897-2

Manufactured in the U.S.A.

All scripture quotations, unless otherwise indicated, are taken from the Holy Bible, New International Version®, NIV®. Copyright ©1973, 1978, 1984 by Biblica, Inc.™ Used by permission of Zondervan. All rights reserved worldwide.

Unless otherwise noted, all Scripture references are from the New Revised Standard Version Bible, copyright 1989, Division of Christian Education of the National Council of the Churches of Christ in the United States of America. Used by permission. All rights reserved.

Contents

Acknowledgments vii
Foreword by Mark D. Baker ix
Introduction: Why Does Anyone Have to Die? xiii

PART ONE: LOOKING FOR ATONEMENT IN OUR STORY

1. Moving from Theory to the Narrative 3

2. Moving from Death toward Resurrection, Forgiveness, and the Kingdom of God 16

3. Is Atonement Only about Death? 19

4. Lenses for Viewing the Atonement 26

5. Finding Ground Zero 36

PART TWO: GROUND ZERO

6. The Sons of Abraham 41

7. The Occupying Forces 63

8. Family, Friends, and Followers 77

9. Jesus of Nazareth 101

PART THREE: METAPHORS AND MEANING

10. Moving the Past toward the Future 109

11. The Death of Jesus and God's Self-Giving Love 117

12. At the Margins of Ground Zero: Preaching the Atonement 124

Conclusion 167
Bibliography 169

Acknowledgments

MY THANKS TO THE faculty at Fuller Theological Seminary, who helped me to start thinking deeply about the atonement during a conference in the winter of 2005; to Dr. Mark Baker, who coached me on the direction of the book, and to Brian McLaren, who introduced me to Mark and encouraged me to share my work with him; to my friend and co-worker Alix Riley, who came up with a creative subtitle; and to my daughter, Laurelin Varieur, who faithfully copyedited the manuscript.

Foreword

DURING THE FIRST SESSION of my Christology course, I tell seminary students that asking questions about the person and work of Christ will lead us to explore mysteries beyond our comprehension. I also say that our probing and exploring might at times challenge some common assumptions about Jesus. I then turn to the whiteboard and write "MORE JESUS, MORE CROSS." I explain that we will not strip away in order to leave them with less, rather the goal of any challenging probe will be to open the way to having a deeper and broader Christology. My hope and prayer is they will end the course having experienced more Jesus and have *more Jesus, more cross* to share with others. I invite you to read this book with the same expectation. As Michael McNichols states in the Introduction, the atonement is not merely a theological concept but a living reality that defies our categories and unravels our attempts at simplification. Let him guide you in some unraveling that will leave you with more Jesus, more cross.

It is common to begin thinking about the atonement by asking about mechanics: *How* did the cross provide salvation? *How* did it *work*? They are appropriate questions, but too often if we start there we also end there. McNichols's starting point is not a theory on the mechanics of atonement. One way he leads us to have *more Jesus* and *more cross* (and more resurrection) is starting by immersing us in the story of Scripture and in the narrative of Jesus' life.

McNichols opens a door to fresh breezes of understanding by inviting us to look at the cross and resurrection through the eyes of others. He takes us to ground zero, the epicenter of salvation, and explores what those who were there experienced and thought. Rather than rushing ahead to a theologian's interpretation from the 3rd century, the 11th or the 21st, letting McNichols guide us in starting our reflection at the cross and resurrection in their historical and biblical context will pay rich dividends.

Foreword

Although giving significant space to the people and events around the cross, this is not historical study just for the sake of historical study. Just as McNichols seeks to return atonement thinking to its proper place, immersed in the biblical narrative, he also seeks to return the atonement to its central place in the Church's mission and ministry. He writes, "How the atonement is communicated in preaching, teaching, and conversation is not incidental to the life of the church or to its mission in the world. Atonement is not an abstract theological concept that belongs only under "A" in a dusty theological dictionary. Atonement is about God, and it draws all hearers into the possibility of new life in and through Jesus."[1]

McNichols urges readers to use the full range of images and metaphors of atonement in the Bible. McNichols adds his voice to many others who also advocate for a multi-faceted understanding and proclamation of the atonement. For McNichols, however, this is not just theoretical. He has done it. Books about the atonement, like this one, are of great importance. But of even greater importance are the images, metaphors, and stories used to communicate the atonement in sermons, in tracts, in evangelistic conversations, in talks to youth around campfires, and in Sunday School lessons. Based on that conviction, I edited *Proclaiming the Scandal of the Cross*. It is a collection of presentations of the atonement using diverse imagery. It was harder to find material for the book than I had expected. A friend connected me with Mike McNichols and suggested that I ask him to contribute to the book. I am deeply grateful for that suggestion. The sermon he sent was a great addition to the collection. Not only did it address a particular theme I was looking for, shame and the cross, it also did a great job of connecting the biblical text to a contemporary context, and used powerful and captivating imagery. McNichols does not just write about the atonement; he can preach it!

The end of this book is a special treasure. After offering some thoughts on how to preach the atonement, McNichols gives us a number of examples of doing so. These sermons lend credibility to his work. He does not just talk about a multi-faceted atonement, he works with different images in each sermon. We can learn a great deal, and borrow from, ways he works with the biblical text, contemporary contexts, and his use of imagery. The sermons are not, however, just an opportunity to learn. May you, through this book, and these sermons experience anew

1. Chapter 12.

the depth and breadth of the saving significance of the cross and resurrection—*more Jesus, more cross*.

Mark D. Baker, PhD
Associate Professor of Mission and Theology
Fresno Pacific Biblical Seminary

Introduction

Why Does Anyone Have to Die?

THE OBVIOUS ANSWER IS that *all* people must ultimately die. The joyful celebration of birth is always shadowed by the grim reality of death. For every new human life that appears, a corresponding grave will be dug. The end of life is a surety, and it is guaranteed that each will have a trajectory of its own.

But the general and abstract acceptance of death is not what really troubles us. It is the death of someone who matters, someone we have come to love and value. It is the death of a cherished person that tears at our hearts and causes us to ask,

Why *this* one? Does this death *mean* something?

We look for meaning in death because we have a difficult time believing that death just happens. We project intentions and purposes onto God in order to explain why our loved one left us too soon, why thousands were swept away by natural disasters, why a person who has contributed generously to others would suffer a wasting disease and then disappear from our midst. We look for answers when we experience these losses, and the rationales offered by well-meaning (and not so well-meaning) people do not generally bring comfort.

It is common for people of faith to attempt theological responses to these questions. Some of these answers suggest things about God that might cause us to wonder if this God is different than Jesus described as the one "who so loved the world" (John 3:16), or as the one characterized in First John as the very essence of love (1 John 4:7–8). We sometimes hear of a God who allows a beloved child to die so that the family will learn some important lessons, or that the death of thousands by tsunami or earthquake is a result of God's retributive wrath, or that God has in mind a greater good that requires the taking of a human life. These responses

Introduction

are often the product of a narrative that is unable to tolerate mystery or to accept the randomness of evil and suffering.

In Luke chapter 13 there is a scene involving some people who ask Jesus about the deaths of some local Jews—one violent episode that occurred at the hands of the local Roman governor, and another tragic accident involving the collapse of a tower. Jesus' response suggests that his questioners were looking for the meaning behind the tragedies:

> He asked them, "Do you think that because these Galileans suffered in this way they were worse sinners than all other Galileans? . . . Or those eighteen who were killed when the tower of Siloam fell on them—do you think that they were worse offenders than all the others living in Jerusalem? (Luke 13:2–4)[1]

Jesus refuses to assign to these losses the deeper meaning that his questioners desire. He merely tells them, in effect, that they too should watch their steps.

It is difficult for us to imagine that the God of the Bible—the God who is filled with love and mission and purpose—would allow anything to occur without reason. After all, either God is in control or he is not. All things must have meaning, otherwise we would be living in a random, chaotic universe, and our lives—lives that we have come to believe are precious to God—are subject to forces that are not God. We have trouble with this, and so we should.[2] Rarely can we get away from the conviction that the cause of something has to be related to its meaning. As Dietrich Bonhoeffer observed,

> All scientific questions can be reduced to two: What is the cause of X? and, What is the meaning of X? The first question embraces the realm of the exact sciences and the second that of the study of the arts; both belong together.[3]

---

1. In John 9:1–3, Jesus' disciples are looking for the meaning behind the suffering of the man who was born blind. They suggest that either the man or his parents, through their own sinful acts, were responsible. Jesus dismisses both suppositions and turns their attention to what God is about to do.

2. We have a biblical precedent for our struggle. Job and his friends spent a great deal of time deliberating over the problem of bad things happening to good people. Job's friends declared that there had to be a reason for Job's suffering, most likely a reason linked to some secret sin of Job's. Job argued that he had done nothing to deserve his troubles, and that the fault for his suffering rested with God. For his part, God showed up at the end of the story with a series of outbursts that offered, in effect, only one answer: *I am God, and you are not.*

3. Bonhoeffer, *Christ the Center*, 28.

Introduction

That people will one day die is a scientific certainty that we can affirm. It is the art that confounds us—in the deaths that matter to us, there has to be some kind of meaning.

There is a theme that the Bible appears to embrace: We humans live in a dangerous, broken world. The desire of God—that all of creation would live in open, unhindered relationship with him—has been countered by humanity's preference for other things. By our own devices we have opened ourselves to all that the forces of the universe can deliver: Natural disasters, hostile environs, the horrors of human sin, the fear of death. In the end we find only the conviction that this state of affairs is not as it should be. There is clearly something wrong with the world.

When it comes to Jesus, the question of his death has fueled theological debates for centuries. The death of one so important, one so pivotal in our perception of human history, cannot easily be explained away as another random and tragic occurrence, especially since there is resurrection to follow. We long for reasons and our reasons craft our theologies about what it means to find the new life that we believe defines us as the people of God. What we conclude about this particular death matters because it speaks significantly about how we see the character of God, his mission in the world, and his destiny for the human race and all of creation.

I began this project in the year 2010 during the season of the church year that is characterized by wonder. It's the time following Advent and Christmas when we are called to marvel at what God has done in the person of Jesus the Christ, the one we first meet as the child of wonder and then watch him meet his death as a crucified Messiah. It is a time when we reimagine the story in fresh and new ways and rehearse it within our ancient traditions. My hope is that we would continue to wonder and marvel at this great mystery that we have come to call The Atonement, seeing it not merely as a theological concept but also as a living reality that defies our categories and unravels our attempts at simplification. It is also a story that must continue to be told.

Michael McNichols
Epiphany 2012

PART ONE

Looking for Atonement in Our Story

1

Moving from Theory to the Narrative

> The English word *atonement* is derived from the two words "at onement" and denotes a state of togetherness and agreement between two people. Atonement presupposes two parties that are estranged, with the act of atonement being the reconciliation of them into a state of harmony.[1]

> Jesus' self-consciousness as the one sent to die confronts us with the central mystery of the vocation of Christ, namely, his calling to be obedient to God's divine mandate to the point of death. Out of Jesus' own self-awareness, therefore, arose the early Christian proclamation that Jesus is the atonement for human sin. How are we to understand this central declaration of our faith? What is the significance of his death? And how does Jesus' sacrifice affect us?[2]

> "But we had hoped that he was the one to redeem Israel."
> (Luke 24:21a)

THE ANCIENT AND ONGOING processes of developing theological reasons for Jesus' death have resulted in a variety of atonement theories. Several have emerged over the centuries, each one finding dominance for a period of time, and then giving way to new theological constructions. When it comes to applying meaning to the death of Jesus, these theories have

1. Ryken, et al, "Atonement," 54.
2. Grenz, *Theology for the Community of God*, 340.

come about through fresh biblical engagement and also through changing cultural grids.[3]

Theological reflection about the death of Jesus should not, however, begin with atonement theories. It should begin by immersion into the story we are given in Scripture about how and why he was killed. Jesus didn't just die—he was executed. He was the victim of political and religious intrigue and was set up to die a criminal's death.[4] Peter makes this clear in his first sermon given on the Day of Pentecost:

> "You that are Israelites, listen to what I have to say: Jesus of Nazareth, a man attested to you by God with deeds of power, wonders, and signs that God did through him among you, as you yourselves know— this man, handed over to you according to the definite plan and foreknowledge of God, you crucified and killed by the hands of those outside the law." (Acts 2:22–23)

In his teachings and through the working of signs and wonders, Jesus disrupted the religious and political status quo. The local Jewish leaders felt threatened by him, fearing that the Roman government would bring harsh correction to actions hinting at revolution. These leaders were also protective of the faith of the Jewish people, and resisted any attempts at altering the religious structures they had come to value. Jesus was a threat at many levels.

For their part, the Romans seemed generally unimpressed by Jesus. There was, of course, the centurion who asked Jesus to heal his servant and then made a profound declaration about faith (Matthew 8:5–10; Luke 7:1–10). Outside of that, no one seemed to be on high alert because of Jesus, even when he entered Jerusalem as the crowds cheered him on. The Romans weren't particularly concerned when they saw a humble, unarmed peasant riding alone into town on a donkey. Insurrectionists rarely took on that kind of posture.

The Romans were, however, happy to oblige the Jewish religious leaders in the end when they demanded that Jesus be put to death. The Romans were good at this sort of thing and believed that the occasional

---

3. Gary Anderson suggests that changes in cultural perspectives are seen in the metaphors employed in Scripture, such as the image of sin as a *weight* in Leviticus (16:21–22) compared to the image of sin as a debt in the Lord's Prayer and in the parable of king who wanted to clear out his accounts (Matthew 18:23–34). Anderson, *Sin: A History*, 6–7.

4. For more extensive exploration of the reasons for Jesus' death, see Wright, *Jesus and the Victory of God*, chapter 12.

Moving from Theory to the Narrative

public execution was helpful for keeping the rabble in order.[5] Watching someone suffer and die on a rough wooden cross would make a person think twice about crossing the Romans. After all, it was Caesar who was Lord.[6]

Up to the point of his arrest, Jesus had impacted many people. He had disciples, friends, family, enemies, and people who watched him from a distance. After his death, how might they have tried to make sense of what had just happened?

∼

On August 31, 1997, Diana, Princess of Wales, was killed in a car crash in Paris, France. Millions of people all over the world mourned her death. Early reports blamed her death on speeding paparazzi. A later investigation suggested that the car's driver was intoxicated.[7]

While Diana's life had its share of scandal, many were saddened that a young, beautiful mother with a long ancestral connection to Britain's Royal Family would die so violently and tragically. Consistent with her international rock-star status, the loss was felt deeply by many people all over the world.

If, however, we were to ask the great *why?* question about her death, we would reach too far if we claimed that Diana had to die in order to satisfy the needs of the British Monarchy, or that her death was orchestrated for a larger purpose that makes her passing meaningful. Instead, we would be better served to turn to some obvious answers: This is what happens to people who ride in a car driven recklessly by an intoxicated driver.

---

5. Joel Green affirms Rome's use of crucifixion in dealing with those who disturbed the peace: ". . . Crucifixion was used in the Roman provinces above all as a deterrent against sedition. By inference, then, we might conclude that Jesus was crucified under Pontius Pilate as an insurrectionist. This inference is supported by the Gospels themselves, for there the issue put before Pilate is clearly one of sedition." Green, "Death of Jesus," 153.

6. "If it were remembered at all from the perspective of Rome, Jesus' death might have been used as an illustration of what happens when the mighty arm of the empire responds to one regarded as a threat to *Pax Romana*." Baker and Green, *Recovering the Scandal of the Cross*, 20.

7. According to the BBC, http://news.bbc.co.uk/onthisday/hi/dates/stories/august/31/newsid_2510000/2510615.stm, accessed 2/13/10.

People would also have to admit that, while Diana's death came too soon, her life passed as all lives must. Death terminates all life on earth. We probably shouldn't be looking for reasons or purposes for Diana's death beyond the obvious. It would be difficult to find greater meaning to her death than what circumstances have demanded. Her death was sad and tragic. But that's just what happens to human beings on planet earth.

∼

We don't usually start with the obvious when we talk about the death of Jesus. We start with our doctrinal grids that have shaped our thinking about what God has done in the person of Jesus. We tend to take theological constructions that have emerged over the centuries and overlay them on the past. Starting with the obvious tends to shake some of those constructions because we are accustomed to starting with our theological preferences rather than with the historic reality of his death. As Abraham Heschel observes,

> Explanation, when regarded as the only goal of inquiry, becomes a substitute for understanding. Imperceptibly it becomes the beginning rather than the end of perception.[8]

The actions of both the Jewish religious leaders and the Romans are the easiest and most obvious answers to the question of Jesus' death: This is what happens when you cross the people who hold the power—they will take you out. In some ways, it is not surprising that this happened, given Israel's history and Jesus' own reflections on the subject:

> "Jerusalem, Jerusalem, the city that kills the prophets and stones those who are sent to it! How often have I desired to gather your children together as a hen gathers her brood under her wings, and you were not willing!" (Matt 23:37)

It had happened before and it would happen again. The prophetic voices that called religious communities to the purposes of God would be silenced when that call violated the preferences of the dominant, ruling culture. Throughout recorded history, people have been killed for calling people to peaceful, healing, and reconciling ways of life.[9] Such calls

---

8. Heschel, *The Prophets*, xxiii.
9. Socrates, John the Baptizer, Ghandi, Martin Luther King, Jr., and Archbishop Oscar Romero, among others.

do not endorse power structures nor do they have a tendency to expand national economies. They do not offer support to the retention of systems that oppress and enslave. Such voices are often silenced. That is why Jesus' enemies intended to silence him.[10] As John Goldingay points out,

> The gospel story is broken-backed. For the first half, Jesus strides the stage like Elijah or Elisha in their heyday, but in the second half, mighty works virtually cease. Jesus is now acted on rather than acting, suffering rather than relieving suffering, abandoned by God rather than working with God. There is a deep illogic about the need for this transition. Why should anyone want to oppose a man who brought people healing, cleansing, deliverance and teaching about questions such as prayer? But that is regularly the destiny of prophets.[11]

We Christians would not say, of course, that the political, religious, and power manipulations by Jesus' enemies have written the end of the story. We believe that the story explodes dramatically soon after Jesus' death, a belief that is grounded in the witness of Scripture. But still the story of his death begins, not with systematic theology, but rather with the account as it is given to us in the New Testament.

In reading Jesus' story in the accounts of Matthew, Mark, Luke, and John, the tendency is to read as though the story is merely chronological, like a transcript of a video recording describing events on a blow-by-blow basis. These accounts, however, were written years after the events they are describing, crafted for particular audiences,[12] and contain important theological reflection, if one reads carefully. These are reflective histories, not attempts at pure, objective, abstraction. The Gospels come to us as the

---

10. As Father Rutilo Grande preached in his 1977 homily just one month before his assassination by an El Salvadoran death squad: "I'm afraid that if Jesus of Nazareth came back, coming down from Galilee to Judea, that is, from Chalatenango to San Salvador, I daresay he would not get as far as Apopa, with his preaching and his actions. They would stop him in Guazapa and jail him there . . . They would accuse him of being a rabble-rouser, a foreign Jew, one confusing the people with strange and exotic ideas . . . They would undoubtedly crucify him again." Wright, *Oscar Romero and the Communion of the Saints*, 42.

11. Goldingay, *Old Testament Theology: Israel's Gospel*, 807.

12. ". . . The Evangelists did not write for the general public but for the Christian groups with which they were associated. Suggestions that the Gospels were composed to fit some fixed lectionary schedule have been judged implausible. But the Gospels were apparently intended for corporate reading and teaching within Christian groups and quickly found a role in their liturgical activities." Hurtado, "Gospel (Genre)," 279.

framing of the writers' ongoing experiences of faith within emerging Christian communities and in light of the larger work of God in Jesus Christ.

Mark's account is the one that is particularly intriguing, because he sneaks up on us. Scholars believe Mark to be the earliest of the four Gospels, possibly written within forty years after Jesus' death. One of the key themes found in Mark is the cluelessness of the disciples—throughout the book they repeatedly fail to catch on to what is happening. This comes out embarrassingly for James and John, whose brash obtuseness is recorded for all of history to enjoy:

> James and John, the sons of Zebedee, came forward to him and said to him, "Teacher, we want you to do for us whatever we ask of you." And he said to them, "What is it you want me to do for you?" And they said to him, "Grant us to sit, one at your right hand and one at your left, in your glory." But Jesus said to them, "You do not know what you are asking. Are you able to drink the cup that I drink, or be baptized with the baptism that I am baptized with?" They replied, "We are able." Then Jesus said to them, "The cup that I drink you will drink; and with the baptism with which I am baptized, you will be baptized; but to sit at my right hand or at my left is not mine to grant, but it is for those for whom it has been prepared." (Mark 10:35–40)

James and John do not understand what is really going on, and Jesus points that out to them.[13] It would be common for people in that time to view the places at the right and left of a ruling monarch to be places of significant power, and these boys wanted to be first in line for those privileges. But Jesus pushes back, making references to drinking the cup and being baptized that don't appear to diminish James's or John's ambitions. He then closes the discussion by declaring that such positions are not in the realm of his authority in the first place; someone else has the power to make those assignments.

I have heard a number of sermons in which it is declared that Jesus is referring to God the Father as the one who holds such power. It may be, however, that such assumptions are based on the same misperceptions that belonged to these sons of Zebedee—that Jesus' mission had something to do with achieving places of power, either on earth or in the

---

13. It's even worse for them in Matthew's version of the story, where their mother makes the request on her sons' behalf (Matt 20:20–28).

heavenly realm somewhere. Mark, in his subtle way, offers a very different, surprising, and scandalous twist to the story. It comes at the end:

> It was nine o'clock in the morning when they crucified him. The inscription of the charge against him read, "The King of the Jews." And with him they crucified two bandits, one on his right and one on his left. (Mark 15:25–27)

Mark appears to connect the dots in a way that underscores the weakness of the assumptions of Jesus' followers. Jesus is indeed recognized as a king, but in a derisive, mocking fashion. It's a big joke to the Romans and a dirty insult to the Jewish leaders. Jesus, the apparently failed Messiah, is dying a criminal's death and is caricaturized as a king. As we survey the scene through Mark's lens we see the irony of the picture. There are the two places to the right and left of Jesus—places previously coveted by James and John—and they are occupied by broken, dying, criminals who join Jesus in this ancient horror show. As the face of the Joker in the *Batman* series offers a dark twist to the innocent silliness of a clown, so does the crucifixion of Jesus provide a murderous parody to the expectation of kingship.

It seems that it was not God who made the royal assignments after all. It was Pontius Pilate, acting as agent for the Roman government. The true right and left on each side of Jesus was not what his followers anticipated. They were looking for power and sovereignty. Instead, they got suffering and death.

In the days surrounding the horrific events of Jesus' crucifixion, what did his followers think? Did they start spinning theories about the theological implications of this tragedy? We are given little evidence for that. What we see are the expressions of grief that would be expected after experiencing such a disillusioning loss:

> Now as they led Him away, they laid hold of a certain man, Simon a Cyrenian, who was coming from the country, and on him they laid the cross that he might bear it after Jesus. And a great multitude of the people followed Him, and women who also mourned and lamented Him. (Luke 23:26–27, NKJV)

> And when all the crowd that came to see the crucifixion saw what had happened, they went home in deep sorrow. (Luke 23:48, NLT)

> Mary stood weeping outside the tomb. (John 20:11)

Can you imagine the grief? His friends, wondering how they might have protected Jesus, how they should have been more devoted than they were, regretting so much and feeling powerless to find a remedy to their pain. His mother would not only grieve the loss of her son, but also the one on whom hope upon hope had been laid. Add to that the betrayal by Judas and his subsequent suicide, and you have more broken dreams than are imaginable.

And from all of that, we try to find meaning.

Perhaps there are no reasons for the death of Jesus beyond the belief that God has orchestrated all these events in order to accomplish his redemptive purposes in the world. Don't we hear that echoed in Peter's Pentecost sermon?

> . . . this man, handed over to you according to the definite plan and foreknowledge of God . . . (Acts 2:23a)

The questions of God's foreknowledge, human free will, and the purposefulness versus randomness of cosmic events have been debated by Christian thinkers for centuries. God's role in the ongoing drama of history has caused many, including the ancient biblical sufferer Job, to give God the credit for both life and death:

> "Naked I came from my mother's womb, and naked shall I return there; the Lord gave, and the Lord has taken away; blessed be the name of the Lord." (Job 1:21)

In the first chapter of Job, there is a theatrical dance between God and the figure of Satan (who is portrayed as a cynical interloper rather than as the dark demon of popular literature) as the subject of Job is discussed. Satan suggests that Job is faithful because God has sheltered him from harm and prospered him. God grants Satan permission to have his way with Job, short of killing him. Soon thereafter, Job is repeatedly struck by disasters. Who, then, is ultimately responsible for Job's suffering? Is it Satan, or is it God? After all, God granted the permission; Satan did not act until that happened.

The ancient Hebrews would have viewed God as the overseer of all things, ranging from blessing to tragedy.[14] Nothing escaped his notice and

---

14. For example, the prophet Amos asks the rhetorical question, "Does disaster befall a city, unless the Lord has done it?" (Amos 3:6b) Also, Hannah makes a similar declaration in 1 Sam 6–8: "The Lord kills and brings to life; he brings down to Sheol and raises up. The Lord makes poor and makes rich; he brings low, he also exalts. He raises up the

he was involved in all of creation. Above all the rulers and dramas that human beings could produce, there was the God of Abraham, Isaac, and Jacob, the true King of all life, and this great King ruled over all things. It could be said that all things were under God's control, even the kingdoms that competed against Israel.

When we say that God is in control, what do we really mean?

A few years ago my wife and I visited some long-time friends in the Pacific Northwest. My friend is a pilot for a major airline and, as a surprise, arranged for us to experience an hour in a flight simulator. It was great fun, and also very instructive to perform take-offs and landings without fear of disaster. I had been under the impression that the huge aircrafts that transport human beings all over the world were completely controlled by the pilots. I imagined the pilots operating the controls of the plane in way that was similar to how I controlled my car when driving it. I was amazed to learn how much of the work of the pilots is actually done by computers rather than by humans. The precision of control exhibited by high-level technology allows thousands of people each day to fly all over the world in relative safety and efficiency.

When we think of control, we can't help but project on God the kind of control we see in our highly-mechanized, technological world. It becomes easy to imagine God as the Divine Air Traffic Controller, sitting at his massive terminal and orchestrating every move on his keyboard and viewing the effects on his cosmic monitor.[15] If God is in control, then perhaps nothing escapes his maneuvering and manipulation, including every step taken by Jesus and every nail hammered into his body.

In the ancient world (and in our world), however, the control of the ruler is always control over a problematic realm. Rome might have been in control of its empire, but there would still be rebellions, insurrections, and wars along the way. While the God of the Hebrews was seen as the ultimate of all rulers, his realm was still a problematic one, born out of the freedom granted to humans to do what they wanted with their lives and for competing kingdoms to make claims of dominance. God was King,

---

poor from the dust; he lifts the needy from the ash heap, to make them sit with princes and inherit a seat of honor. For the pillars of the earth are the Lord's, and on them he has set the world."

15. I am reminded of Gary Larson's *The Far Side* cartoon, showing God hovering over his computer key board while watching the antics of a sinner on the monitor, preparing to hit the "smite" button.

but his subjects were always up to something that would get them into trouble, and many of them were downright rebellious.

But God sees all of that, doesn't he? After all, since God is all-knowing, then he sees every frail, broken move that humans make and has laid it all out long before the creation of the earth. Doesn't God see the past, present, and future all at the same time? God must have orchestrated everything, including the movements of Jesus, in order to accomplish his plan of redemption. Isn't that how things like foreknowledge and control work?[16]

Let's consider this from a different angle. First, we need to stop and entertain the possibility that there is no such thing as *the future*. That is not to say, as far as God is concerned, there is nothing coming down the pike, so to speak. It is, rather, to suggest that the future is not a pre-scripted realm over which God hovers like a time-liberated helicopter.[17] Instead, the future may be nothing more than the constantly-unfolding present that rapidly becomes the past. What gives us hope may not be that the intricacies of the future are predetermined, but rather that all of human life and history is oriented toward God's intentions.

I offer a very limited illustration: If I call my friend and arrange for him to meet me for coffee at 3:00 in the afternoon, then it becomes my intention to make that date. Between the early morning and 3:00, any number of things might take place that push and pull my activities one direction and another. I continue, however, to watch the time, because my responses to those things are now framed by my intention to meet my friend. This illustration breaks down, of course, because something may occur prior to 3:00 to derail my plans completely, regardless of my goal for the afternoon.

The Bible reveals God's ultimate intentions—intentions that will not, regardless of human dramas, be derailed—often in dramatic and powerful language. For example:

---

16. The relationship of God to time is complex and multidimensional. For a detailed discussion on the topic, see Paul Helm, et al, *God and Time: Four Views* (Downers Grove: IVP Academic, 2001). For a challenging approach to the nature of God in relation to time and human experience, see Clark Pinnock, *The Openness of God: A Biblical Challenge to the Traditional Understanding of God* (Downers Grove: IVP Academic, 1994).

17. Nor is it a dimension that co-exists with the past and present and can be visited by means of a DeLorean equipped with a fully-functioning flux capacitor. See the *Back To The Future* trilogy for details.

Moving from Theory to the Narrative

> The wolf shall live with the lamb, the leopard shall lie down with the kid, the calf and the lion and the fatling together, and a little child shall lead them. The cow and the bear shall graze, their young shall lie down together; and the lion shall eat straw like the ox. The nursing child shall play over the hole of the asp, and the weaned child shall put its hand on the adder's den. They will not hurt or destroy on all my holy mountain; for the earth will be full of the knowledge of the Lord as the waters cover the sea. (Isa 11:6–9)

> Then afterwards I will pour out my spirit on all flesh; your sons and your daughters shall prophesy, your old men shall dream dreams, and your young men shall see visions. Even on the male and female slaves, in those days, I will pour out my spirit. I will show portents in the heavens and on the earth, blood and fire and columns of smoke. The sun shall be turned to darkness, and the moon to blood, before the great and terrible day of the Lord comes. Then everyone who calls on the name of the Lord shall be saved; for in Mount Zion and in Jerusalem there shall be those who escape, as the Lord has said, and among the survivors shall be those whom the Lord calls. (Joel 2:28–32)

> Then I saw a new heaven and a new earth; for the first heaven and the first earth had passed away, and the sea was no more. And I saw the holy city, the new Jerusalem, coming down out of heaven from God, prepared as a bride adorned for her husband. And I heard a loud voice from the throne saying, "See, the home of God is among mortals. He will dwell with them; they will be his peoples, and God himself will be with them; he will wipe every tear from their eyes. Death will be no more; mourning and crying and pain will be no more, for the first things have passed away."

> And the one who was seated on the throne said, "See, I am making all things new." (Rev 21:1–5a)

The movement of time into what we call the future might be how human history unfolds as it aims—whether human beings realize it or not—toward the purposes and intentions of God.[18] God's foreknowledge

---

18. The fulfillment of God's purposes is not the same as God orchestrating the movement of all things, nor are God's ultimate purposes divorced from contemporary human experiences in the world. In exploring the New Testament book of Revelation, Richard Bauckham describes how John's visions relate to the historical context in which which he wrote: "The effect of John's visions, one might say, is to expand his readers' world, both spatially (into heaven) and temporally (into the eschatological future), or, to put

may be akin to the way a brilliant physicist might be able to accurately predict the movement of objects given weight, outside forces, trajectory and velocity. God sees all the movements of the universe and sees where all of them will go. Those movements might shift and change over time, but none of them will derail his ultimate purposes and intentions for all of creation.

Assurance of God's faithfulness to his own purposes permeates the very first chapters of the Bible. At the beginning of the book of Genesis (chapters one and two), all that God makes is good. All of creation—including the first humans—lived in an unhindered relationship with God. By chapter three, however, everything appears to unravel. The people turn from God's purposes and seek their own way, unleashing fear and alienation upon the earth. Strangely enough, God does not wipe the people out for their failure, but rather meets them in their broken state.[19] The writer of Genesis then describes a series of attempts to restart what God originally intended for the world.

First, Adam and Eve reproduce ("with the help of the Lord" - Gen 4:1). While the text does not describe their dreams for their children, we might speculate that Adam and Eve would have hoped that the next generation would repair what they had damaged. But in short order their sons engage in conflict and a new enterprise is invented: Murder—a practice that is honed to a fine skill by the time of Lamech, who boasts,

> "I have killed a man for wounding me, a young man for striking me. If Cain is avenged sevenfold, truly Lamech seventy-sevenfold." (Gen 4:24b-24)

Second, all life on the earth is wiped out by a great flood, and a remnant of people and animals are given the chance to start the human experiment anew. Noah and his family survive the flood and re-establish a place on dry land. Before long, however, Noah gets drunk on wine from

---

it another way, to open their world to divine transcendence. The bounds which Roman power and ideology set to the readers' world are broken open and that world is seen as open to the greater purpose of its transcendent Creator and Lord. It is not that the here-and-now are left behind in an escape into heaven or the eschatological future, but that the here-and-now look quite different when they are opened to transcendence." Bauckham, *The Theology of the Book of Revelation*, 7–8.

19. When the people embrace shame for the first time and recognize their own nakedness, God eases their pain by giving them new clothing ("garments of skins" - Gen 3:21).

his vineyard and ends up cursing his own son (Gen 9:25–27). The fracturing of human relationships continues and the new beginning is no better than the old.

Third, the now-expanded population unites to celebrate human ingenuity by building a new city with an impressive tower in its center, one that would have "its top in the heavens" (Gen 11:4). Surely their common language and skills in engineering will result in a unity that will create heaven on earth. Instead, the people are scattered, their language confused, and the project is abandoned.

These three significant experiments fail to re-establish God's intentions for the world. Human involvement and initiation in each case results in disaster. From chapter three through chapter eleven of the book of Genesis, it appears that God's purposes have been thwarted. This is not a picture of a God who knows how to properly orchestrate events, if a God of complete control is what is desired.

Something astonishing happens, however, at the beginning of chapter twelve. God takes the initiative and reaches out to a wandering nomad named Abram, and calls him to a new destiny. There will indeed be a new start for the earth and God's purposes will be fulfilled, but in a way that is different from the beginning. God will work through a particular people—the descendants of Abram—to create a new nation through which "all the families of the earth shall be blessed" (Gen 12:3).

The disasters, of course, do not end with chapter 12.[20] There will be international conflicts, defections to false gods, betrayals, faithlessness, exile, and legalism. Yet, God's purposes remain intact and are supremely expressed in the person of Jesus. At the end of all things, God promises a new heaven and a new earth, when all he has purposed will be fulfilled. From the beginning to the end, however, things will get quite messy.

---

20. As Walter Brueggemann points out, the way forward for Israel later comes through Moses after the Exodus: "The narrative account of reality stretches wondrously from creation, that daring moment of first light in the midst of darkness, when elemental confusion began to take ordered form that made life possible. The story moves through one of the world's great dysfunctional families (in Genesis) through the slave camp of Egypt, through the desperate hunger of wilderness, all the way to Sinai. And there, out of the very mouth of God, is disclosed an alternative way to order the world." Brueggemann, *The Word That Redescribes the World*, 46.

2

Moving from Death toward Resurrection, Forgiveness, and the Kingdom of God

> I Believe in God, the Father almighty, creator of heaven and earth. I believe in Jesus Christ, his only Son, our Lord. He was conceived by the power of the Holy Spirit and born of the Virgin Mary. He suffered under Pontius Pilate, was crucified, died, and was buried. He descended to the dead. On the third day he rose again. He ascended into heaven, and is seated at the right hand of the Father. He will come again to judge the living and the dead.[1]

THIS STATEMENT OF BELIEF from the Apostles' Creed provides a doctrine of the atonement that is derived from the narrative of Scripture and has informed Christian thinking for 1,800 years. It draws its authority from the witness of the early church and, as a testimony of faith, is straightforward and sparse in interpretation, telling both the church and the world pointedly *that* Jesus lived, suffered, died, and rose. What it doesn't offer is an explanation of *why*.

In the Gospel of Luke, Jesus spends considerable time with his friends after the resurrection. Seeing Jesus whole and alive after his execution surely brought wonder as well as comfort to the remnant that had been grieving his death. All we are told by Luke is that Jesus explained what it meant to be the Messiah, gave his followers the assignment to

---

1. http://anglicansonline.org/basics/apostles.html, accessed 8/17/10.

announce God's forgiveness, and helped them see how this all relates to the kingdom of God.

> Then he said to them, "These are my words that I spoke to you while I was still with you—that everything written about me in the law of Moses, the prophets, and the psalms must be fulfilled." Then he opened their minds to understand the Scriptures, and he said to them, "Thus it is written, that the Messiah is to suffer and to rise from the dead on the third day, and that repentance and forgiveness of sins is to be proclaimed in his name to all nations, beginning from Jerusalem." (Luke 24:44–47)

> After his suffering he presented himself alive to them by many convincing proofs, appearing to them over the course of forty days and speaking about the kingdom of God. (Acts 1:3)[2]

For all the drama that had just taken place, one would think that there would be some explanation about why Jesus had to die in this way. Instead, the focus that Luke offers is on resurrection, forgiveness, and the coming of God's kingdom. In the sequel to his Gospel, Luke continues these themes through the sermon that Peter preaches to the gathered Jewish pilgrims on the day of Pentecost:

> "You that are Israelites, listen to what I have to say: Jesus of Nazareth, a man attested to you by God with deeds of power, wonders, and signs that God did through him among you, as you yourselves know—this man, handed over to you according to the definite plan and foreknowledge of God, you crucified and killed by the hands of those outside the law. But God raised him up, having freed him from death, because it was impossible for him to be held in its power. . . This Jesus God raised up, and of that all of us are witnesses. Being therefore exalted at the right hand of God, and having received from the Father the promise of the Holy Spirit, he has poured out this that you both see and hear. . . Therefore let the entire house of Israel know with certainty that God has made him both Lord and Messiah, this Jesus whom you crucified." (Acts 2:22–24, 32–33, 36)

---

2. Most Protestant churches celebrate Easter as a single-day event, while the larger calendar of the Christian year spreads Easter out over seven Sundays (called Eastertide), perhaps in recognition of the forty days that Jesus spent with his followers after his resurrection. Tradition suggests that reflecting on something as astonishing and significant as the resurrection of Jesus should require something more than a single early-morning church service and an Easter egg hunt.

Peter is not shy about casting blame for Jesus' death on the Jewish worshippers who had made their pilgrimage to Jerusalem for the feast of Pentecost. He doesn't let the Romans—people he refers to as ones "outside the law"—off the hook completely, but sees them as instruments of the people who conspired to kill Jesus in the first place. Even after that, Peter declares that the plan didn't work, because God has raised Jesus from the dead, confirming that the true Messiah and Lord is Jesus.

The argument is fairly tight as it is based on what Peter and the others actually experienced with Jesus. They saw him die, they knew who was responsible for that death, they encountered the resurrected Jesus, listened to him as he connected all the dots for them, and then were astonished by the surprising work of the Holy Spirit. Peter is heavy on witness, but rather light on theological interpretation, even though he suggests that what happened to Jesus was not outside of God's purview:

> ". . . this man, handed over to you according to the definite plan and foreknowledge of God, you crucified and killed by the hands of those outside the law." (Acts 2:23)

After that, the book of Acts is filled with the action of people swept up by the power of the Holy Spirit, giving themselves over to God's ongoing work in the world. The early Christians' firm belief in the resurrection of Jesus and the powerful presence of the Holy Spirit was enough to launch them into a bold missionary effort that cost many of them their lives.

In those early days, however, no one seemed to ask *why* Jesus had to die[3]—at least, the accounts of the Gospels and Acts do not offer to us such conversations as those.[4] The people appeared to take the reasons for Jesus' death at face value. He died because some people killed him, even though, as Peter points out, this death was somehow wrapped up in God's purposes. It was an unjust death, perpetrated by evil people, and it created yet another murderous stain on the nation of Israel. But Jesus didn't stay dead and now their lives—and the world—would never be the same.

---

3. ". . . Neither the New Testament nor the Christian tradition has seen fit to articulate in a univocal manner *how* Christ redeems us for our sins. The creeds make clear that Christ died for humanity but say nothing about how his death atones." Anderson, *Sin: A History*, 193.

4. In his review of the New Testament data, Gustaf Aulén concludes: ". . . The New Testament teaching corresponds with that of the early church; it being understood that there is not to be found in either case a developed theological doctrine of the Atonement, but rather an idea or *motif* expressed with many variations of outward form." Aulén, *Christus Victor*, 78.

3

Is Atonement Only about Death?

> Atonement theology starts with violence, namely the killing of Jesus. The commonplace assumption is that something good happened, namely the salvation of sinners, when or because Jesus was killed. It follows that the doctrine of atonement then explains how and why Christians believe that the death of Jesus—the killing of Jesus—resulted in the salvation of sinful humankind.[1]

THE SCENE: A YOUNG vicar, trapped by precocious young children during a wedding reception, is attempting to respond to their questions about the reason for Jesus' death. Young Ben has been ruthless in his questioning; his little sister, Karen, offers insightful and penetrating footnotes. Ben doesn't understand why Jesus didn't just shape-shift and blast all the Romans to keep them from killing him. Karen listens attentively to the vicar's answer.

> Vicar: "It was the way that God chose. He wanted to sacrifice his only son. He wanted to show us how important it was. So he chose the most precious thing in the world to him. The most precious thing in the world to him was Jesus."
>
> Karen: "Then why did he kill him?"
>
> Vicar: [Silence][2]

---

1. Weaver, *The Nonviolent Atonement*, 2.
2. "Awkward Questions About Jesus," from the British TV Series *Outnumbered*.

Atonement at Ground Zero

In spite of the evidence implicating the Jewish religious elite along with the Romans, people still want the death of Jesus to have come because of God's orchestration. As the poor Vicar quickly learned, the theory suffers under scrutiny, especially at the hands of young, bright children who refuse to take the things adults say at face value. Any five-year-old will tell you that it doesn't make sense to kill what you love. If God truly loved Jesus and then sentenced him to a horrible death, then what are the implications of God loving you or me?

But the theologies that put God the Father and Jesus the Son into a tragic, sacrificial destiny are persistent. I once overheard someone tell a young man who was seeking answers about faith that Jesus was killed because God needed a death to satisfy his anger at sin. While I (and the young man) found this explanation to be difficult and problematic, it is one that has held a position of prominence for many years.

The story, however, follows a rhythm that finds a place in our minds. The great and powerful God has been offended, and there must be a form of retribution in order for the divine anger to be appeased. There must be an acceptable sacrifice in order for the cosmic balance to be restored. The ones who have brought the offense are disqualified from such sacrifice, since their own violations have made them unclean in the sight of the divine presence. So it must be an innocent, one untouched by the sin of the others. That one must die so that appeasement will be made and the offending masses will find forgiveness.

It is a familiar story. It is the story of the Incas, who sacrificed children to the god of the volcano.[3] It is the story played out comically in the Tom Hanks movie, *Joe vs. the Volcano*.[4] But is it the story of the Bible? Is it the story of the Gospel? Is it *our* story?

While recognizing the costliness of forgiveness, Richard John Neuhaus also identifies the problem with the language we use to describe God's forgiveness in relation to Jesus:

> Forgiveness costs. Forgiveness costs dearly. Some theories of atonement say that Christ paid the price. His death appeased

http://www.youtube.com/watch?v=WQak6ng0RXQ. Clip accessed 2/14/10.

3. For recent findings on the subject, see Mark Henderson's article, "Incas fattened up their children before sacrifice on the volcano," *TimesOnLine*. http://www.timesonline.co.uk/tol/news/world/us_and_americas/article2570682.ece. Accessed 2/15/10.

4. *Joe vs the Volcano*. DVD. Directed by John Patrick Shanley. 1990; Warner Brothers Pictures.

Is Atonement Only about Death?

God's wrath and satisfied God's justice. That way of putting it appeals to biblical witness and venerable tradition, and no doubt contains great truth. Yet for many in the past and at present that way of speaking poses great problems. The subtlety of the theory is overwhelmed by the cartoon picture of an angry Father who demands the death of his Son, maybe even kills his Son, in order to appease his own wrath. In its vulgar form—which means the form most common—it is a matter of settling scores, a drama vengeful and vindictive, more worthy of *The Godfather* than of the Father of whom it is said, "God is Love."[5]

If the God of the Bible is different from the god of the volcano, then why would anyone's death—particularly the death of Jesus—be part of God's purposes? Does God really *need* death in order to do what he wants to do in the world? Is there some principle of justice that hovers over God, insisting that he do things in a certain way in order to balance the cosmos? If that is the case, then who is calling the shots: The God of the Bible or the power of justice that requires certain responses from him? We can accept that God saw it all coming, but the idea that death would need to factor into God's intentions for redeeming the world creates problems for us—not just in abstract theology, but in the way we view the very character of God.

The theory of appeasement or satisfaction is one idea among several that attempts to make sense of what happened to Jesus. In thinking about God's larger purpose for the human race, it makes sense that people throughout the ages would try to assign purpose to the specific act of Jesus' death. If God had a plan, then Jesus' death had to be a part of the plan. That's the logic.

Again, it might help to start with the obvious. While Jesus died at the hands of his enemies, the ending of his physical life was always inevitable. It was inevitable that Jesus would die for the same reason that all human beings—all living things, for that matter—ultimately die. Jesus died because he was born.

Some might argue that the Christian belief in the dual nature of Christ—both human and divine—changes the plane of existence when it comes to Jesus. If his conception came at the initiation of God, then doesn't it follow that his death could only come the same way—that Jesus would not be subject to the same trajectory of life and death that plagues

5. Neuhaus, *Death on a Friday Afternoon*, 10.

all human beings? The Bible, however, does not offer this idea to us. In the narrative we see Jesus born as all humans are born; he grows and we see him again at age twelve; he then appears to us at age thirty and dies three years later. His life follows the same developmental pathway that is the destiny of all people. There is no suggestion in Scripture that the avoidance of the cross would have insured earthly immortality for Jesus.

There is also a way of thinking about Jesus' death on the cross that suggests the possibility of failure on God's part, and it goes something like this: If the cross had not been the instrument that resulted in the death of Jesus, then God's plan of salvation would have collapsed. Had Jesus not been brutally murdered, then God would have failed in his grand adventure. In some way, it might be said, God needed the specificity of the cross in order to accomplish his great plan of salvation.

In our Trinitarian framework, we think of Jesus being fully God as well as fully human. It's a mystery to us, even as we try to make sense of it. Yet, we have the words of our Scriptures that affirm this divine/human phenomenon:

> In the beginning was the Word, and the Word was with God, and Word was God. (John 1:1)

> And the Word became flesh and lived among us, and we have seen his glory, the glory as of a father's only son, full of grace and truth. (John 1:14)

> Let the same mind be in you that was in Christ Jesus, who though he was in the form of God, did not regard equality with God as something to be exploited, but emptied himself, taking the form of a slave, being born in human likeness. (Philippians 2:5–7a)

> He is the image of the invisible God, the firstborn of all creation; for in him all things in heaven and on earth were created, things visible and invisible, whether thrones or dominions or rulers or powers—all things have been created through him and for him. . . . For in him all the fullness of God was pleased to dwell . . . (Colossians 1:15–17, 19)

If the fullness of God was living in Jesus, if he was truly *the Word*—the very Word of God who has created all things—*become flesh*, then that fullness was in him at conception. When God inhabits flesh—when God is *born*, in the human sense of the word—then it is inevitable that God will experience human death. Whether that death comes at age thirty-three

Is Atonement Only about Death?

on a rough Roman cross or at age ninety-nine in bed at home, this death will come by virtue of birth.[6]

When it came to fully identifying with human beings, fully engaging with all the struggles, pain, suffering, life, joy, hope, and ultimate death, God immersed himself in the human race in the birth of Jesus. It was a guarantee that Jesus, once out of the womb, would come into a world where all the powers of reality—including sin and death—would have their way with him. This oft-repeated prayer affirms that the entirety of Jesus' life and death is wrapped up in God's plan of reconciliation:

> Holy and gracious Father: In your infinite love you made us for yourself; and, when we had fallen into sin and become subject to evil and death, you, in your mercy, sent Jesus Christ, your only and eternal Son, to share our human nature, to live and die as one of us, to reconcile us to you, the God and Father of all.[7]

The mystery of the incarnation was part of the challenge some early Christians faced in attempting to understand what was going on with Jesus.[8] Some claimed that, if he was truly one with God, then he couldn't really have suffered and died like a regular person. He must have only *appeared* to have endured all those things. At least, that's what one of the prevailing philosophies of the day suggested.[9] So people tried to fit Jesus into that scheme. John, who gave us the pastoral letters of First, Second, and Third John, addressed this by affirming the reality of Jesus as a true human being who suffered and died:

> We declare to you what was from the beginning, what we have heard, what we have seen with our eyes, what we have looked at and touched with our hands, concerning the word of life— this life was revealed, and we have seen it and testify to it, and declare

---

6. Ray Anderson affirms God's complete embrace of human life as the heart of the atonement: "The atonement, as a vicarious death of Jesus Christ on the cross, is part of a larger context of reconciliation that stretches from Bethlehem to Calvary and the resurrection. When God assumed humanity as a form of being through the incarnation, he assumed an estranged humanity, under the judgment of death." Anderson, *On Being Human*, 173.

7. *Book of Common Prayer*, 362.

8. Often the result was the creation of various heresies, described by Rachel Muers as ". . . somebody trying to make things too tidy, refusing to take theological risks." Muers, "Adoptionism," 54.

9. While the heresy of Docetism became prominent in the second century, its roots lie in Platonic thought that preceded it. Ibid., 24–25.

> to you the eternal life that was with the Father and was revealed to us— we declare to you what we have seen and heard so that you also may have fellowship with us; and truly our fellowship is with the Father and with his Son Jesus Christ. (1 John 1:1–3)

We believe—and most historians agree—that Jesus was a real person who was born roughly 2,000 years ago in Palestine and was executed by the Romans at age thirty-three. We can grasp the fundamental idea that people who are born will one day die, and marvel at the thought that God would submit himself to such a temporal process. Yes, the cross was the instrument used to facilitate Jesus' death, but one day he would have died as all people do. For Jesus to enter human existence without the inevitability of death would be for God to engage in a partial incarnation. God, in the person of Jesus, fully identifies with all humans in the complete cycle of human life. Why, then, the emphasis on the cross and death, not only in our theologies of atonement but also in our Scriptures? Here are some examples from the Bible:

> For Christ did not send me to baptize but to proclaim the gospel, and not with eloquent wisdom, so that the cross of Christ might not be emptied of its power. For the message about the cross is foolishness to those who are perishing, but to us who are being saved it is the power of God. (1 Cor 1:17–18)

> . . . We proclaim Christ crucified, a stumbling-block to Jews and foolishness to Gentiles . . . (1 Cor 1:23)

> For I decided to know nothing among you except Jesus Christ, and him crucified. (1 Cor 2:2)

> May I never boast of anything except the cross of our Lord Jesus Christ, by which the world has been crucified to me, and I to the world. (Gal 6:14)

> He has abolished the law with its commandments and ordinances, so that he might create in himself one new humanity in place of the two, thus making peace, and might reconcile both groups to God in one body through the cross, thus putting to death that hostility through it. (Eph 2:15–16)

> . . . through [Jesus] God was pleased to reconcile to himself all things, whether on earth or in heaven, by making peace through the blood of his cross. (Col 1:20)

> And when you were dead in trespasses and the uncircumcision of your flesh, God made you alive together with him, when he forgave us all our trespasses, erasing the record that stood against us with its legal demands. He set this aside, nailing it to the cross. (Col 2:13–14)

> ... we do see Jesus, who for a little while was made lower than the angels, now crowned with glory and honor because of the suffering of death, so that by the grace of God he might taste death for everyone. (Heb 2:9)

It is clear from the New Testament letters (particularly those attributed to the apostle Paul) that the cross of Jesus stands for something important in the thinking of the early church, and therefore it remains important for us as well. However, for people to focus only on the death of Jesus on that cross as the single, pivotal point in all of God's dealing with the human race might be the equivalent of mourning through Good Friday but never celebrating Easter. We have more than enough texts of Scripture to point us to how we live our lives as persons in community, the hope that we have in Jesus' resurrection, and the confidence that we have in God's forgiving, reconciling love.

For the witnesses to Jesus' execution, his death might have seemed pivotal, but in a way that would be different from the perspective we have on this side of history. On the Friday of his death through the early Sunday morning of his resurrection, the shift in reality would not seem like a move from trespass to forgiveness. It would seem like the dashing of hopes and dreams, the failure of another would-be Messiah, and the reestablishment of the status quo. Our Scriptures, along with our imaginations, may help us consider what Jesus' death meant to the earliest players in this great drama.

But, first, what are the various theological lenses through which we typically view the significance of the death of Jesus? There are many, but only a few that have been dominant at different times and for different reasons.

4

Lenses for Viewing the Atonement

> What can wash away my sin?
> Nothing but the blood of Jesus.
> What can make me whole again?
> Nothing but the blood of Jesus.[1]
>
> I heard about His groaning,
> Of His precious blood's atoning,
> Then I repented of my sins
> And won the victory.[2]
>
> Lives again our glorious King, Alleluia!
> Where, O death, is now thy sting? Alleluia!
> Once He died our souls to save, Alleluia!
> Where thy victory, O grave? Alleluia![3]
>
> Every one of us deserves to die.[4]

∼

IMAGES OF THE ATONEMENT appear in varied forms in Christian hymnody and pop music. They seem to move from guilt to sacrifice to appropriation to victory without conflict or hesitation, and sometimes within

---

1. Robert Lowry, "Nothing But the Blood of Jesus," 1876. Public Domain.
2. Eugene Monroe Bartlett Sr., "Victory in Jesus," 1939. Public Domain.
3. Charles Wesley, "Christ the Lord is Risen Today," 1739. Public Domain.
4. Brenton Brown, "Thank You for the Cross," Vineyard Songs (UK/Eire), 2001.

Lenses for Viewing the Atonement

the same pieces of music. Grace must be granted to the songwriters and present-day psalmists, however, for echoing a multiplicity of sometimes-conflicting interpretations of the death of Jesus. These musicians stand in a long line of thinkers, writers, and singers who have tried to capture in words and images the meaning of Jesus' death which are expressed in a mosaic of expressions. We can probably thank the apostle Paul for starting the whole visual journey:

> What then are we to say about these things? If God is for us, who is against us? He who did not withhold his own Son, but gave him up for all of us, will he not with him also give us everything else? Who will bring any charge against God's elect? It is God who justifies. Who is to condemn? It is Christ Jesus, who died, yes, who was raised, who is at the right hand of God, who indeed intercedes for us. Who will separate us from the love of Christ? Will hardship, or distress, or persecution, or famine, or nakedness, or peril, or sword? As it is written, "For your sake we are being killed all day long; we are accounted as sheep to be slaughtered." No, in all these things we are more than conquerors through him who loved us. For I am convinced that neither death, nor life, nor angels, nor rulers, nor things present, nor things to come, nor powers, nor height, nor depth, nor anything else in all creation, will be able to separate us from the love of God in Christ Jesus our Lord. (Rom 8:31–39)

Consider the combination of images: God doesn't withhold his own son, which somehow translates into God's generosity toward human beings (the image of a loving father); as such, no charge can be brought against God's elect[5] because God has already made everything right for those who trust in Jesus (the image of a law court); Jesus is now at God's right hand (the image of the king's throne room), interceding for all of us in prayer; because of Jesus, there is nothing that can separate God's people from his love—not earthly things (the image of contemporary persecution and oppression) nor things outside of the earth (the image of

---

5. Newbigin sees the elect, not as those chosen to the exclusion of the world, but rather those chosen for the sake and blessing of the world (Newbigin, *The Open Secret*, 25). Lohfink agrees, and sees the elect people of God as a sign to the nations of the world: "The election of a single people from the many nations does not imply preference for one over the others or discrimination against the others in favor of the chosen one; election of one people takes place *for the sake of the others*. The chosen people is to become a sign to the other peoples of what God plans to do with the world as a whole." Lohfink, *Jesus and Community*, 138.

supernatural realities like angels and "powers"). Thinking about the death and resurrection of Jesus requires many images and metaphors because of the complex nature of the implications that God, in the person of Jesus the Christ, would suffer and die.[6]

The more time that passed from the actual events of Jesus' death, the more opportunity people had to speculate on the deeper meaning of it all. They would move from ancient Jewish imagery (that people like the apostle Paul might favor) to Greco-Roman logic, medieval caste systems, and strong judicial frameworks. In each era of development, the contexts of the day offered new ways of thinking about this mysterious phenomenon that we call the atonement.[7]

THE DEATH OF JESUS AS GOD'S VICTORY OVER SIN, DEATH, AND SATAN

Imagine living a hundred or so years after the events of Jesus. Any human witnesses would be dead and gone, but letters such as those written by Paul to the Corinthians would have circulated widely among the emerging Christian church. Paul's citing of Hosea 13:14 in his great statement about God's victory through Jesus would have stirred up plenty of theological conversation:

> "Death has been swallowed up in victory. Where, O death, is your victory? Where, O death, is your sting?" The sting of death is sin, and the power of sin is the law. But thanks be to God, who gives us the victory through our Lord Jesus Christ. (1 Cor 15:55–58)

---

6. Recognizing that the Bible often employs metaphor to convey the deep realities of God is not to say that there is no real connection with those realities. Lawley and Tompkins helpfully describe this connective process: "Metaphors correspond in a special way to the original experience they are describing—through isomorphism. In other words, the form of a metaphor is *different* from the original experience, but it has a *similar* organisation. This means that the attributes of its symbols, the relationships between symbols and the logic of the whole matches the organisation of what is being described. While there will be some correspondence of tangible components, the key role of metaphor is to capture the essence, the intangible, the relationships, and the patterns." Lawley and Tompkins, *Metaphors in Mind*, 7.

7. For extensive explanations of the various historic theories of the atonement, see Gustav Aulén, *Christus Victor: An Historical Study of the Three Main Types of the Idea of the Atonement*; Baker and Green, *Recovering the Scandal of the Cross*; Hans Boersma, *Violence, Hospitality, and the Cross: Reappropriating the Atonement Tradition*; and J. Denny Weaver, *The Nonviolent Atonement*.

Clearly, in Jesus' resurrection, death gets cheated out of its ultimate power. But what is death when we speak of it as though it is a living being? People would speculate about this and come up with a creative way to think about what was happening behind all the obvious circumstances of Jesus' death. If, in Jesus, God somehow defeated death, then there had to be something going on in the unseen world—the world of principalities and powers.

Irenaeus, the second-century Bishop of Lyons, saw the incarnation as key to the atonement and developed the idea of recapitulation, i.e. God reverses the effect of Adam's sin by representing the human race in Jesus. In that unseen, cosmic undoing, humanity is restored to the place of God's intention:[8]

> When he became incarnate and was made man, he began anew the long line of human beings. And he furnished us . . . with salvation—so that what we had lost in Adam (namely, to be in the image and likeness of God), we might recover in Christ Jesus.[9]

The third-century Christian thinker Origen is credited with putting some strong imagery to this way of thinking, retaining Irenaeus's focus on the incarnation but also speculating about what happened behind the scenes between the crucifixion and the resurrection. It goes something like this: When Adam and Eve submitted to the serpent's deception, they effectively sold all of humanity into the clutches of Satan. In defiance of God, Satan was holding the entire world ransom, and freedom could only be had when a ransom price was paid. In order to rescue the human race from Satan, God offered to exchange his son, Jesus, for the entire human race. As Origen declared:

> Christ is our redemption because we had become prisoners and needed ransoming.[10]

---

8 "In recapitulation Christ both sums up and restores humanity. Irenaeus placed great importance on the incarnation—Christ becoming human so that he could fill the representative role and so that he could pass through every stage of life. Adam lived making wrong choices, but Christ lived making right choices. Christ as a human could both resist and conquer the devil, where the human Adam did not." Baker and Green, *Recovering the Scandal of the Cross*, 145.

9. Bercot, *A Dictionary of Early Christian Beliefs*, 43.

10. Ibid., 45.

Satan readily agreed to God's offer, believing that he would forever hold some power over God by imprisoning God's son. However, the goodness of Jesus was more than Satan could tolerate, so he gave Jesus up to death, laughing at the destruction this would bring to God. However, God tricked Satan in the resurrection, because Satan didn't realize that death could not hold onto Jesus. So, in the end, God rescued both Jesus and the world from the hands of the devil.

In Origen's day the concept of the ransom was grounded in real-life occurrences. It was not uncommon for criminals in that time to kidnap travelers and demand a price before the captives would be released. That the imagery surrounding the idea of ransom would find its way into the developing Christian theology of the day is not entirely surprising.

While the description of God and Satan wrapped up in the intrigue of kidnapping and ransom payment might seem odd to us, there is an inner logic to the story that is reasonable. If Jesus was truly raised from the dead, then both sin and death were defeated—cheated, in a way, out of what was normally their due. Sin—the power of evil—did indeed have its way with Jesus, and death sealed Jesus' fate, or so it seemed. In the resurrection, the powers of sin and death that were observed by the witnesses were rendered ultimately powerless. Yes, evil—through sinful people—nailed Jesus to the cross. Yes, death—violent and bloody, but still the fate that awaits all humans—closed his eyes and shut off his breath. But both lost their power of finality when Jesus was raised. Projecting that onto a hidden, spiritual battle between God and Satan was actually some very creative theological innovation.

The fourth-century apocryphal document *The Acts of Pilate* offers a behind-the-scenes look at Jesus' death. In that creative account, Satan is gleefully attempting to deliver Jesus into the hands of Hell (portrayed as a being who rules the underworld, the place of the dead) and describes Jesus' crimes as undoing all the disease, pain, and suffering that Satan has inflicted upon the world. Upon learning the true identity of Jesus as "the King of glory," and in hearing the shouts from heaven praising Jesus, Hell refuses to capture Jesus in death, and instead turns the tables on Satan by making death his eternal home. In this ancient drama, the work of God in Christ is seen as victory over both Satan and the power of death. In this striking passage, Hell chastises Satan for his blunder:

> Thou wouldest crucify the King of glory and at his decease didst promise us great spoils of his death: like a fool thou knewest not what thou didst. For behold now, this Jesus putteth to flight by the brightness of his majesty all the darkness of death, and hath broken the strong depths of the prisons, and let out the prisoners and loosed them that were bound. And all that were sighing in our torments do rejoice against us, and at their prayers our dominions are vanquished and our realms conquered, and now no nation of men feareth us any more.[11]

For the earliest theologians of the church, victory over sin and death permeated their thinking about the atonement. It would be later that images from the western world would offer other ways of considering what God had done in and through Jesus Christ.

THE DEATH OF JESUS AS AN OFFENSE AGAINST GOD

Did God really owe something to Satan in order to buy back the human race? Is God really a deceiver who would trick even the devil? About a thousand years ago, Anselm of Canterbury claimed that the "Ransom to Satan" theory had too many holes in it to be plausible. Instead, in efforts toward both theological credibility and contemporary relevance, he looked to images of his time to help flesh out the difficulties of the theory of the atonement.

In Anselm's day, the ruling class controlled the daily lives of the peasant class. Land barons and lords oversaw vast estates that were worked by serfs who labored, lived, and died at the pleasure of their rulers. On occasion, a peasant might do something that would offend the local ruler. When that happened, there had to be some sort of compensation to satisfy the wounded honor of the ruler. It was unthinkable that such offenses would go without a required payment being made.[12]

---

11. James, *The Gospel of Nicodemus, or The Acts of Pilate*, "Descent into Hell," VII.

12. "According to the patronal ethics of Anselm's feudal world, a lord and his vassals lived in peace at the intersection of reciprocal obligations. The lord provided capital and protection, the vassal loyalty and tribute. In this microworld, social order depended on honoring and serving the landowner. Within this cultural environment, God is presented by Anselm as a feudal lord, and this within a larger criminal-justice framework that may seem alien to us. The legal system in the United States is oriented around punishment of the guilty; in Anselm's day, however, the working of justice depended first on satisfaction, paying what was due." Carroll and Green, *The Death of Jesus in Early Christianity*, 261.

Atonement at Ground Zero

Anselm tried to capture the atonement in his own contemporary images: Just as the local ruler required satisfaction in order for an offense to be forgiven, so does God require satisfaction in order for the offense of human sin to be forgiven. It would have been improbable in Anselm's day that forgiveness would be granted without compensation that exceeded the value of the offense. The only proper price for offending God is death, since God's honor cannot be satisfied with money, land, or any other form of human tribute. But God cannot be satisfied by just any death—after all, the deaths of the sinful humans who caused the offense in the first place would hardly do, since they all end up dying anyway. It is only the death of an innocent, pure person that could satisfy God's damaged honor. Such a person is only found in the Son of God, Jesus. Jesus dies in the place of humans, taking care of God's need for satisfaction. The debt that the human race owes to God—a debt that has thrown off the moral balance of the universe—is satisfied in Jesus' death.[13]

Again, there is value to be found here. In Genesis chapters one and two, we see God's gracious, creative work as the world, plants, animals, and humans are brought into being. It's all seen as good, yet in chapter three it all comes crashing down because of human defiance. God reacts in anger (but also in graciousness, meeting the people in their new, broken state of existence), so clearly he was unhappy about all that was good being trampled upon. Indeed, human sin and rebellion are offenses against God.

Anselm's concept of compensation, however, is limited because it is framed in the feudal system of his day. While Anselm would understand the death of Jesus as God's full participation in that death, over time the theory has been seen as forcing God the Father and Jesus the Son into an adversarial relationship, in which God requires his son's death in order to satisfy the offense of human sin.[14]

---

13. While the roots of the satisfaction theory precede Anselm, he is often credited for its development. "Needless to say, it is not implied that Anselm's teaching was wholly original. The stone lay ready to hand; but it was he who erected them into a monumental building." Aulén, *Christus Victor*, 2. Also, the contemporary church at large tends to skip over Abelard's "moral influence" view, developed at about the same time.

14. Gary Anderson clarifies the difference between Anselm's theological thinking and the way his views on the Atonement have been reinterpreted in contemporary thought. He shows how Anselm did not see the death of Jesus as an act of God that required the death of an innocent in the place of the guilty human race. Instead, Anselm saw Jesus' death as a voluntary, salvific act. "Anselm could hardly be more explicit—Christ does

THE DEATH OF JESUS AND GOD'S REQUIREMENT FOR JUSTICE

The western post-Reformation church has tended to hold tightly to the theory of the atonement known as *penal substitution*: The sin of humanity has struck at the heart of God's inherent justice, an offense that requires nothing less than death. God sends Jesus to suffer that death on behalf of the human race, thereby satisfying God's requirement for justice.[15] In effect, Jesus substitutes for the human race which deserves only death in order to balance the scales of justice. This view is similar to the satisfaction motif generally attributed to Anselm, but is more grounded in the western view of justice than in the medieval view of honor.

Regardless of the defense of a particular theory of the atonement, each remains just that: A theory.[16] By nature, a theory abstracts itself away from reality (whether by intention or by necessity) in order to develop conceptual grids about a subject. As N. T. Wright observes,

> ... Theories of atonement are all, in themselves, *abstractions* from the real events. The events—the flesh-and-blood, time-and-space happenings—are the reality which the theories are trying to understand but cannot replace.[17]

The dominant theme in all theories of the atonement is Jesus and the events given to the church through the writings of the New Testament.[18]

---

not atone for the sins of humankind by becoming a penal substitute. He suffered death solely of his own choosing in order to redeem the human race. His divine Father took no pleasure or delight in the fact of his suffering or death." Anderson, *Sin: A History*, 197.

15. This appears to be particularly dominant in the West: "... The popularity of the penal-satisfaction model of the atonement has less to do with exegesis and historical theology and more to do with the cultural narrative in the West, with its emphases on individualism and mechanism." Green and Baker, 42.

16. This is not to diminish the importance of the New Testament's exploration of the meaning of the death of Jesus, particularly in Hebrews and in the writings of Paul. Both, however, do use multiple images to frame their understanding.

17. Wright, *Evil and the Justice of God*, 94.

18. The full narrative of Scripture is key to atonement theory. As William Placher observes, "... What is most basic to Christian faith is not, for example, any soteriological theory or even doctrines about the triune God or the two-natured person of Christ but rather the stories of God's covenant work with Israel and then the birth, life, death and resurrection of Jesus Christ. We figure out and affirm the doctrines necessary to make sense of those stories (holding them tight if they really are necessary), but the stories come first." Placher, *How Does Jesus Save?*, 26.

Yet, the view of the atonement that dominates western thinking is one that focuses primarily on Jesus' death on a cross (utilizing the theory of penal substitution). We can affirm, with the late John Stott, the centrality of the death of Jesus when he claims, "There is then, it is safe to say, no Christianity without the cross,"[19] because we believe in the cross as a historic reality. The narrative of Scripture would also allow us to affirm: *There is no Christianity without Jesus.*[20]

There are places in southern California where I have studied, prayed, and worshipped that display life-sized, bronze statues of Jesus at different moments of his life. At Point Loma Nazarene University in San Diego there is a sculpture of Jesus calling Peter to leave his nets and follow him—an expression of that institution's value of Christian service; at the Vineyard Christian Fellowship in Anaheim there is Jesus washing Peter's feet—a reflection of that faith movement's desire to serve the church and the world; at Mater Dolorosa retreat center in Sierra Madre is a depiction of Jesus carrying his cross to Golgotha while his mother, Mary, reaches out to him—an image that captures that center's focus on the sufferings of Jesus and the suffering of the world; at Fuller Theological Seminary in Pasadena a startling ground-level sculpture shows Jesus being nailed to the cross by two men—a reminder of the historic reality of Jesus' crucifixion; and at the Mission in Santa Barbara Jesus stands placidly next to Mary, the first to discover him after his resurrection—assuring each visitor that the hope of the world did not die with Jesus on the cross.

Each of these bronze renderings reflects something important about Jesus while simultaneously expressing a value that is part of the essential identity of a particular group of people. Yet it is unlikely that anyone would make the claim that the sculpture they own tells the whole story of Jesus. No single, artistic depiction can capture all that the Bible tells about Jesus.

In a similar way, no single theory of the atonement can capture all that the Bible teaches about the significance of Jesus' death.[21] Each

---

19. Stott, *The Cross of Christ*, 68.

20. In speaking of Jesus I am referring to both the historic Jesus of the gospel narratives and also the risen, ascended Jesus who continues to be present in and through the Holy Spirit.

21. In his introduction to McKnight's *The King Jesus Gospel*, N. T. Wright observes the overall limitations that people have in viewing Christianity as a whole: "The Christian faith is kaleidoscopic, and most of us are color-blind. It is multidimensional, and

Lenses for Viewing the Atonement

theory might be seen as a different lens through which Jesus is viewed from distinct historical viewpoints. While people might camp on one view or another as the only way to understand the significance of Jesus' death, history tells us that there have been a variety of pathways in the attempts to grasp something that deeply challenges our limited powers of comprehension.[22]

So we can push back through the years, sorting out how these various theories of the atonement came to be, but it is important that we keeping pushing—past the Reformation, past the medieval era, past the church councils, and land in close proximity to the actual events of Jesus' death and resurrection. Before we camp on a theory, we need to begin at the beginning.

---

most of us manage to hold at most two dimensions in our heads at any one time. It is symphonic, and we can just about whistle one of the tunes." Wright, "Introduction," in *The King Jesus Gospel*, 11.

22. Carroll and Green point out the limitations of metaphor when attempting to create a theory of the atonement: "Metaphors are two-edged: they reveal and conceal, highlight and hide. This means, first, that no one metaphor will capture the reality of the atonement. Metaphors from Israel's sacrificial system communicate something important about the death of Jesus, but they cannot contain the profundity of the cross of Christ." Carroll and Green, *The Death of Jesus in Early Christianity*, 262. Brevard Childs extends this to the way that ancient Israel viewed atonement in the Old Testament: "I am far from certain that the community of Israel restricted the meaning of sacrifice to only one theory of atonement. The detailed descriptions serve the function of excluding unacceptable, that is, pagan vestiges, but without providing full propositional clarity. Therefore, a range of possible interpretations seems to have been retained." Childs, *Biblical Theology of the Old and New Testaments*, 505.

5

Finding Ground Zero

The term *ground zero* may be used to describe the point on the Earth's surface where an explosion occurs. In the case of an explosion above the ground, *ground zero* refers to the point on the ground directly below an explosion.[1]

It was now about noon, and darkness came over the whole land until three in the afternoon, while the sun's light failed; and the curtain of the temple was torn in two. Then Jesus, crying with a loud voice, said, "Father, into your hands I commend my spirit." Having said this, he breathed his last. (Luke 23:44–46)

MAJOR DISASTERS ON EARTH usually have a spot that is termed "ground zero." There is a monument in the Japanese city of Nagasaki that marks the location where an atomic bomb detonated in August 1945. The plot of land that was once home to the Twin Towers of the World Trade Center in New York City became ground zero after the terrorist attacks of September 11, 2001. After a major earthquake, the epicenter is sometimes referred to as ground zero. When an epidemic breaks out, researchers try to determine ground zero—the place where it all began.

Studying ground zero is helpful because it draws researchers back to the first cause or impact of a significant disaster or event. There are, however, limitations that will plague the various research projects. First,

---

1. http://en.wikipedia.org/wiki/Ground_zero. Accessed 7/5/10.

Finding Ground Zero

all ground zeroes are based on events of the past. As such, they cannot be filmed or chronicled or texted as they occur. Therefore, researchers will have to deal with the effects of changes in the environment, weighing their scientific assumptions against the evidence that they encounter, and dealing with uncertainties about key facts in the occurrences. In some cases, the disasters are so devastating that there are no surviving eyewitnesses to what actually happened. Second, the debris left by the disaster has to be sorted through in order to get a reasonably clear picture of what has occurred. Some of the wreckage is helpful in reconstructing the facts of the event while some is just the residual detritus.

For Christians (and even for many who do not hold an affinity to Christianity), the moment when Jesus died is history's ground zero. We would claim that everything has changed since that event and that its significance is cosmic in its scope. Two thousand years of theological rumination have offered up numerous ways of thinking about Jesus' death, but there still remains a ground zero that precedes all theological reflection. But like the other ground zeroes of human experience, we approach this one with limitations. We have no film or on-the-spot transcript that gives us the details we seek. There are no living eyewitnesses to Jesus' death. We are hampered by cultural and historical rubble that is sometimes helpful and sometimes not. We also bring to our search a worldview that is 2,000 years beyond the event itself, creating a lens through which we gaze that will inevitably distort our conclusions. But we do have something that draws us into close proximity with this particular ground zero.

We have the witness of Scripture.[2]

One of the reasons why the texts that we refer to as the Gospels and Acts have been so carefully guarded over the centuries is that they contain the accounts of the eyewitnesses of the events surrounding the life

---

2. While offering caution about ignoring the difference between the first century, Mediterranean world in which the New Testament documents emerged, and the character of the contemporary age in which we live, Carroll and Green suggest that we approach our texts by ". . . respecting the integrity of the various NT writings, accepting their invitations to enter into their worlds and to adopt a perspective from within these writings. We appreciate how the writers sought to communicate in language appropriate to their life situations, while at the same time we leave ourselves open to being challenged by their visions of reality and the purpose of God. This requires that we decenter our own self-interests so as to be addressed by the text as 'other,' to allow it to engage us in creative discourse, and to take the risk of being shaped, indeed transformed, in the encounter." Carroll and Green, *The Death of Jesus in Early Christianity*, 275.

of Jesus and the subsequent emergence of the church. As Christians we believe these witnesses to be truthful, and through them we hear the voice of God.

We also hear authentic witness in the failures, misunderstandings, betrayals, and thickheadedness of the people surrounding Jesus. The Scriptures ring true to us in every confession of fault that the Gospel writers refused to sidestep. The sheer *humanness* of the story causes the reader to relate in his or her own stumbling faith, recognizing that those who have gone before us have never quite gotten it right, but often have lurched their way into faithfulness by the very grace of God.

In the following section, three groups of early eyewitnesses will be profiled. Scripture will inform this process, but there will be, admittedly, some speculation added and some imagination required. Without living witnesses to interview, some assumptions will have to be made based on what can be sorted through at this epic ground zero. With all of our present-day limitations, we approach three groups who were at or close to Jesus' ground zero: The sons of Abraham, the occupying forces, and the family, friends, and followers of Jesus. Our fourth investigation will be with Jesus himself as he experienced his own death firsthand.

PART TWO

Ground Zero

6

The Sons of Abraham

NICODEMUS

Now there was a Pharisee named Nicodemus, a leader of the Jews. He came to Jesus by night and said to him, "Rabbi, we know that you are a teacher who has come from God; for no one can do these signs that you do apart from the presence of God." Jesus answered him, "Very truly, I tell you, no one can see the kingdom of God without being born from above." Nicodemus said to him, "How can anyone be born after having grown old? Can one enter a second time into the mother's womb and be born?" Jesus answered, "Very truly, I tell you, no one can enter the kingdom of God without being born of water and Spirit. What is born of the flesh is flesh, and what is born of the Spirit is spirit. Do not be astonished that I said to you, 'You must be born from above.' The wind blows where it chooses, and you hear the sound of it, but you do not know where it comes from or where it goes. So it is with everyone who is born of the Spirit." Nicodemus said to him, "How can these things be?" Jesus answered him, "Are you a teacher of Israel, and yet you do not understand these things?" (John 3:1–10)

Then the temple police went back to the chief priests and Pharisees, who asked them, "Why did you not arrest him?" The police answered, "Never has anyone spoken like this!" Then the Pharisees replied, "Surely you have not been deceived too, have you? Has any one of the authorities or of the Pharisees believed in him? But this crowd, which does not know the law—they are accursed." Nicodemus, who had gone to Jesus before, and who was one of them, asked, "Our law does not judge people without first giving them a hearing to find out what they are doing, does it?" They replied, "Surely you are not also from Galilee, are you? Search and you will see that no prophet is to arise from Galilee." (John 7:45–52)

After these things, Joseph of Arimathea, who was a disciple of Jesus, though a secret one because of his fear of the Jews, asked Pilate to let him take away the body of Jesus. Pilate gave him permission; so he came and removed his body. Nicodemus, who had at first come to Jesus by night, also came, bringing a mixture of myrrh and aloes, weighing about a hundred pounds. They took the body of Jesus and wrapped it with the spices in linen cloths, according to the burial custom of the Jews. (John 19:38–40)

∽

NICODEMUS AND JOSEPH OF Arimathea were not big risk-takers. They were drawn to Jesus and even followed him, but they did so secretly (John describes Joseph as a disciple, but only refers to Nicodemus as the one "who had at first come to Jesus by night." Either John assumed Nicodemus's status as a disciple, or he was suggesting that Nicodemus was not as close a follower as Joseph).[1] They were both members of the Sanhedrin, the ruling Jewish council and supreme court of Israel. With all the controversy and drama surrounding Jesus, exposing their affinity toward him could be costly. In the midst of their clandestine care of Jesus' crucified body, we are given no record of a conversation between them. Perhaps their grief consumed their ability to speak. Their minds, however, would have been active, mixing suffering and grief with love and scraps of memory.

The conversation relayed in John chapter 3 might have been rattling around in Nicodemus's head. Jesus had spoken of being "born from above" (or, "born anew" or "born again"). It was a puzzling exchange, with Nicodemus inquiring and then wrestling with Jesus' imagery. Nicodemus was a well-educated Jewish leader, yet none of this was making sense to him. As a Pharisee, he would have been interested in Jesus, not only because of his miraculous works, but also with questions about his

---

1. In an apocryphal New Testament document, written between the second and fourth centuries, Nicodemus is portrayed more boldly than in the canonical Gospels. He not only pleads Jesus' case to Pilate, but also stands up to the Sanhedrin. James, *The Gospel of Nicodemus, or The Acts of Pilate*, V/I.

loyalty to the traditions of Israel.² Jesus' call to be born from above, born in a new way by the Spirit of God, would have challenged Nicodemus's orthodox sensibilities and his questioning of Jesus would be a natural reaction to someone in his position. At the same time, Jesus must have impacted Nicodemus deeply because his interest in Jesus later turned into intimate devotion as he and Joseph tenderly cared for Jesus' ravaged body.

As Nicodemus looked upon the corpse of the one who had forfeited his life as had many prophets before him, he would surely have wondered about the validity of Jesus' words regarding new birth. Nicodemus might have believed that something new had occurred in his own life and that what Jesus said offered hope to all of Israel, but the herald of that idea now lay dead before him. Perhaps the words seemed empty to him now. It would be difficult to look at the dead body of Jesus and continue the idea of being born anew.

But the story of the new birth conversation found its way to John somehow, who is the only Gospel writer who offers the account. It might be that, years later, the elder statesmen John and Nicodemus reflected on that long-ago conversation, or John may have heard about it directly from Jesus. Either way, the exchange remains somewhat cryptic, especially to twenty-first century minds.

Nicodemus seems to have been both confused and offended by Jesus. The confusion would lie not only with the mysterious language of new birth, but also with the way Jesus seems to play fast and loose with pronouns. At first, both of them seem to be speaking generally—Jesus claiming that "no one" can see the kingdom without being born from above (just as Nicodemus observes that "no one" can do miraculous signs without God's presence), and then Nicodemus objecting that it is impossible for "anyone" to return to a mother's womb to repeat the birth process. Then Jesus narrows the conversation, speaking in such a way that it sounds like it's all about Nicodemus and his need to be rebirthed. Jesus then seems to widen the scope of his meaning as his pronoun usage shifts the focus from the singular to the plural.

We don't typically catch this kind of subtle change in English, since the pronoun *you* is used as both a singular and plural form.³ If a teach-

---

2. As N. T. Wright affirms, "The Pharisees saw themselves as standing firm for the old ways, the traditions of Israel, against paganism from without and assimilation from within." Wright, *The New Testament and the People of God*, 187.

3. Unless you are from the southern US, where "ya'll" and "all ya'll " helps with that

er tells one student something, she might say, "You must turn in your assignment by 3:00." But she could say exactly the same words to a classroom of 30 students, including all of them in the statement, making *you* a plural pronoun. Context would drive the interpretation, but the word *you* would remain the same.

The Greek language originally used in the Gospel of John offers that distinction. Jesus is quoted as saying,

"Do not be astonished that I said to *you* . . .'" (singular)

"'*You* must be born from above.'" (plural)

While we often read this as a personal, individually focused statement, the pronoun is clearly plural. When Jesus speaks of the need to be "born from above," he appears to be speaking about more than just Nicodemus. While the conversation is about Nicodemus, it isn't only about him. There is a larger body of people that Jesus must have in mind. That's where the offense comes in.

As Nicodemus packed herbs and spices on Jesus' body and secured them tightly against the dead skin with strips of linen cloth, he might have revisited that moment of offense:

"Are you a teacher of Israel, and yet you do not understand these things?"

What things—the absurd idea of being born a second time? What did that have to do with being a teacher of Israel? Nicodemus was a leader and a man of distinction. He was, indeed, a teacher of Israel, and yet Jesus claimed that he had missed something that was, to Jesus, obvious. What Nicodemus was missing was not something about only him, but about the entire nation of Israel, the people of God.

Both Nicodemus and Joseph of Arimethea shared more in common than their devotion to this crucified, failed Messiah. They were leaders of Israel and, as such, served as Israel's representatives in two ways: They would represent the concerns of the people to the Sanhedrin, and they would represent the values and priorities of Israel back to the people. In a way similar to contemporary business brokers who represent both buyers and sellers as their agents, both Nicodemus and Joseph were agents of Israel.

The intention behind using the plural "you" could be to indicate that all of Israel, the people of God, represented in that secret meeting by the

---

distinction.

Pharisee Nicodemus, needed a new birth. In order to truly embrace their identity as God's people, a people loved by God and set apart by him for the blessing and benefit of the entire world,[4] Israel would need to be reborn, not in the usual way, but in a way generated by the Spirit of God. Perhaps, after his meeting with Jesus, Nicodemus would reimagine his role as a teacher of Israel.

Through his tears, after Jesus died, Nicodemus might have wrestled with those words in a new and tragic way. His own kinsmen, his fellow leaders of Israel, the very agents of the people of God, had seen to the death of Jesus, who clearly had lived his life in the very presence and fullness of God. Jesus was not the guilty one—it was the Sanhedrin that was guilty of murder. It was that ruling Jewish council, of which Nicodemus was a member, that had committed a crime that should have been punishable by death. But once dead, they and the nation they represented would have to stay dead. There could be no new birth for them unless it would come in a way that defied their rational expectations.

There is not much information available about Nicodemus beyond the events described in the New Testament. Legend suggests that he continued as a disciple of Jesus and was later martyred. The Gospels do not describe his ouster from the Sanhedrin, even though his colleagues chastised him for defending Jesus. Nicodemus would have to return to his role as a leader and teacher of Israel, and continue to serve as a member of the Sanhedrin. He would look into the eyes of the others and remember that they conspired to murder the one he had loved. When they sought to cover up the story of the resurrection with tales of body snatching, he would trust his life to the risen Lord. If Nicodemus remained a member of the Sanhedrin, he would undoubtedly struggle with his relationships with the group. Their differences were now more than disputes about theology or law. While Nicodemus would have certainly rejoiced in the vindication that God brought in Jesus' resurrection, he would still remember that his fellow Jewish leaders had acted unjustly.

---

4. See Genesis 12 and 22 for the initial call to Abram that would set the DNA for the people of God.

CAIAPHAS

> Many of the Jews therefore, who had come with Mary and had seen what Jesus did, believed in him. But some of them went to the Pharisees and told them what he had done. So the chief priests and the Pharisees called a meeting of the council, and said, "What are we to do? This man is performing many signs. If we let him go on like this, everyone will believe in him, and the Romans will come and destroy both our holy place and our nation." But one of them, Caiaphas, who was high priest that year, said to them, "You know nothing at all! You do not understand that it is better for you to have one man die for the people than to have the whole nation destroyed." He did not say this on his own, but being high priest that year he prophesied that Jesus was about to die for the nation, and not for the nation only, but to gather into one the dispersed children of God. So from that day on they planned to put him to death. (John 11:45–53)

~

It has been said that teenage drivers have sharper reaction skills than older drivers, but that older drivers have fewer accidents because of their ability to anticipate traffic problems and to take in the whole picture of the road. Teenage drivers might be able to zip in and out of traffic faster than their parents, but the kids bang up their cars (and their bodies) with greater frequency because they often do not see the larger traffic picture as it unfolds before them. It seems to boil down to the wideness of one's view.

Bringing a dead man back to life would be big news anywhere, and it would surely have hit the front page of the *Jerusalem Times* after Jesus raised Lazarus from the dead in Bethany. Those in close proximity to the event were like teenage drivers captured by the moment, filled with explosive emotion, and overflowing with the joy of life. All that the people could see was what stood before them—a man who had died and was buried days earlier now standing whole and alive, breathing in the air and embracing his loved ones. Even those who ran back from Bethany to Jerusalem to report to the Pharisees what had happened were astonished by what they had witnessed.

The council members were also riveted to the moment, but in a dark sense of panic. They couldn't seem to appreciate the enormity of the event except to the extent that it might disrupt the status quo and cause the occupying forces of Rome to destroy all that was precious to Israel. If the miracles continued, they reasoned, Rome might feel threatened. When that happened, retribution was swift and sure, and many would hang from crosses before the machinery of power and dominance ran out of steam.

Caiaphas the High Priest had a broader, more reflective view. He seemed to understand the concept of representation or substitution— it would be better for the Jews to allow Rome to execute one person who would stand in the place of the nation of Israel rather than to allow these foreign oppressors to wipe out the nation itself. It was in the interests of both Israel and Rome for that to happen: For Israel, substituting one trouble-maker would be a small price to pay for self-preservation; for Rome, making the example of the one as a warning to the many was part and parcel of their methodology of control. As Joel Green observes,

> Roman practices were guided by their interest in the deterrent value of crucifixion. Quintilian (c. A.D. 35–90s) observed that, "whenever we crucify the guilty, the most crowded roads are chosen, where most people can see and be moved by this fear. For penalties relate not so much to retribution as to their exemplary effect" (*Declamationes* 274). Variation in the manner of how victims were affixed to the cross would have served not only as sadistic entertainment but also the need to leave the victim alive as long as possible for maximum deterrent effect."[5]

The leaders of Israel came to believe that substituting a victim would save the nation from Rome's retribution; the Roman leaders used substitution as a means of operating the machinery of oppression.

The High Priest was considered a powerful person in the life of Israel. Rome recognized that power as well, and created political bridges that would require Israel to keep its own people in line. Caiaphas served in his role as high priest for eighteen years—ten of those years under Pontius Pilate—and to survive so long in that role would require strategic political astuteness. Caiaphas was cagey enough to understand the dynamics of representational sacrifice, and he would be the chief architect of the plan to assign Jesus to that sacrificial role. In doing that he would satisfy not only the Romans, but also his Jewish associates who were disturbed by Jesus.

Caiaphas would surely have remembered the stories that had been passed down about the mass crucifixions of 800 Jewish rebels fifty years earlier. The Jewish ruler Alexander Jannaeus didn't rely on substitution to

---

5. Green, "Kaleidoscopic View," 158.

quell a rebellion; he destroyed all who were implicated, and the blood had flowed freely on that dark day. Even though his fellow Jews condemned the action, the corporate memory of that horror would remind the people of Caiaphas's day that the ruling powers of that era could exact retribution on a mass scale if it suited their purposes. Caiaphas would want to avoid a revisiting of that scene during his watch.

By finding a way to hand Jesus over to the Romans as a potential insurrectionist, Caiaphas would be tapping into the power of representation. He would prove to Rome that he could successfully guide the people of Israel by handing over one of his own countrymen as a substitute for the sin that could so easily surface when people forgot their place in the world. The wrath of Rome would be satisfied even before it exploded, and the perceived safety and peace of Israel would remain in tact. Letting the powers of evil—powers that were built into Rome's global dominance—have their way with this one man would discharge the pressure of control that needed periodic release.[6]

Giving up one man to death for the sake of the nation was a politically astute strategy, and Caiaphas had no doubt that he would be successful. It was, after all, his duty as a religious leader to make this happen. In the death of Jesus, wrath would be averted. It was a familiar and powerful wrath—it was the wrath of Rome, one that always demanded appeasement.

Caiaphas would have still been in this role as High Priest as the church began to emerge. Persecutions of the first post-Pentecost Christians would have come during his era of leadership.[7] It must have angered Caiaphas, thinking that he had resolved the Jesus problem by orchestrating his death, to have his followers so boldly embark on their missionary endeavors following the so-called resurrection of Jesus. Perhaps his failure to control the new Jesus movement was part of his removal from office only a year or so later.

---

6. Kraus sees Jesus' representative role in Israel as the key to interpreting the accusations made by his opponents: "Indeed, a real part of the accusation against [Jesus] was his mingling with 'publicans and sinners.' In the eyes of his accusers he was contaminated by his intimate association with them. This representational intimacy gave the accusation of blasphemy much of its force. His identification with the multitudes underscored the absurdity and danger of his claims in the eyes of the leaders. It also made the crowds more vulnerable to his presumed delusion. Thus they concluded that he must die rather than have the whole nation perish in delusion (John 18:14). In this sense he took the place of the Jewish nation as a representative substitute." Kraus, *Jesus Christ Our Lord*, 215.

7. Reilly, "Joseph Caiaphas."

THE CROWDS

> So [Jesus'] fame spread throughout all Syria, and they brought to him all the sick, those who were afflicted with various diseases and pains, demoniacs, epileptics, and paralytics, and he cured them. And great crowds followed him from Galilee, the Decapolis, Jerusalem, Judea, and from beyond the Jordan. When Jesus saw the crowds, he went up the mountain; and after he sat down, his disciples came to him. Then he began to speak, and taught them, saying: "Blessed are the poor in spirit, for theirs is the kingdom of heaven." (Matt 4:24—5:3)
>
> When [Jesus] saw the crowds, he had compassion for them, because they were harassed and helpless, like sheep without a shepherd. (Matt 9:36)
>
> And there was considerable complaining about [Jesus] among the crowds. While some were saying, "He is a good man," others were saying, "No, he is deceiving the crowd." (John 7:12)
>
> So Pilate, wishing to satisfy the crowd, released Barabbas for them; and after flogging Jesus, he handed him over to be crucified. (Mark 15:15)
>
> Then the people as a whole answered, "His blood be on us and on our children!" (Matt 27:25)
>
> And when all the crowds who had gathered there for this spectacle saw what had taken place, they returned home, beating their breasts. (Luke 23:48)

Crowds are fickle. They can pack out sports stadiums in order to enjoy a few hours of athletic competition, and then end the day with violence, injury and death when the wrong team wins. Rock stars attract them like flies to honey, only to find themselves, years later, abandoned by their fans and reduced to playing county fairs and oldies concerts. Crowds fill mega-church sanctuaries, but drift away when certain religious itches are no longer scratched.

One of the most well-known crowds in US memory is the one that gathered in upstate New York from August 15th to the 18th in 1969. The Woodstock music festival was seen as a pivotal moment in time, not only because of the showcasing of many rock musicians, but also because the

500,000 young people who gathered for their fill of sex, drugs, and rock 'n roll remained, for the most part, peaceful. It was seen as a social phenomenon that might have marked a dramatic change in American society.

Less than four months later, the Altamont Free Concert in northern California—headlined by the Rolling Stones, policed by the Hell's Angels, and anticipated as a west coast version of Woodstock—was characterized by violence and murder. 300,000 people gathered for this event (perhaps even some who had been at Woodstock) only to find that the illusion of a new and peaceful world was shattered by violent reality.[8]

Yes, crowds can be fickle.

Jesus' reference to the crowds as "sheep without a shepherd" had a scriptural precedent (Num 27:17, 1 Kgs 22:17, 2 Chr 18:16, Isa 13:14). The people of Israel had long been seen by the prophets as a lost people who had forgotten their identity as the people of God. Jesus' observation, however, was not one of condemnation or mockery, but rather of compassion that resulted in him bringing healing to their lives. And as he healed, cast out demons, and raised people from the dead, the crowds gathered.

When Matthew describes the gathering of the crowds in the account that has come to be called "The Sermon on the Mount," (Matt 4:23—6:29) he paints a dramatic picture. The crowds are made up of people from a variety of locales, ranging from Jerusalem all the way out to the land "beyond the Jordan." Jesus performs some astounding miracles and people continue to be drawn as if by a magnet. Jesus sees the crowds, and then ascends the mountain where his disciples join him. Imagine Jesus sitting on the incline just above his disciples so that he can look out over their heads and see the people—so many lost, hurting, broken people—as he speaks out each proclamation of blessing on behalf of

- The poor in spirit
- Those who mourn
- The meek
- Those who hunger and thirst for righteousness
- The merciful
- The pure in heart

---

8. For a cultural analysis of these two events, see Michael Walker, *Laurel Canyon: The Inside Story of Rock and Roll's Legendary Neighborhood*, 128–138.

- The peacemakers
- The persecuted

Each category of persons is followed by words of blessing. Was Jesus abstractly listing a new ethical law that would make demands on his followers, or was he describing to his disciples what he saw in the crowds? Certainly his words offer a new framework of life for his followers that not only dives deeply into the human heart, but also releases people into a rich and generous life. At the same time, in this portrait of blessing that Matthew gives to us, Jesus seems to be enacting in real time what God had promised to do through the great ancestor Abraham:

> "I will make of you a great nation, and I will bless you, and make your name great, so that you will be a blessing. I will bless those who bless you, and the one who curses you I will curse; and in you all the families of the earth shall be blessed." (Gen 12:2–3)

Indeed, the people received blessing from Jesus, the One who embodied all that Israel should have been. They came to him as the marginalized ones because their afflictions would characterize them as anything but blessed. These broken people were brought or accompanied by faithful family and friends who would have seen to it that their loved ones encountered Jesus. He bestowed on them more than mere words; he healed their bodies, scattered demonic forces, and re-identified them as God's beloved—his blessed ones.

Something, however, happened along the way. Certainly some of the people would have gone home rejoicing and thanking God, while others might have become part of the crowd that fringed the twelve disciples. How many of them morphed into the mob that demanded Jesus' death, we do not know. But we do know from the story that the overwhelming attitude of the crowds toward Jesus shifted from praising him with shouts of "Hosannah!"[9] as he entered the city on a donkey to screaming for his blood to be on their hands.

Was there, perhaps, both an individual and corporate forgetfulness that came when the crowds—possibly fueled by the work of Sanhedrin-backed thugs—started calling out for Jesus' death? What happened to the memories of deep and liberating teachings, of physical healings, exorcisms and the raising of the dead to life? In mob environments, a sense of

---

9. Matt 21:1–11, Mark 11:1–11, Luke 19:28–40, John 12:12–19.

self is often lost as personal identity becomes swallowed in the corporate identity of the mob.[10] That phenomenon may have been taking place with the people of Jerusalem. Now this new, death-demanding crowd had moved from a people *blessed* to a people that *cursed* their own Messiah.

Once the nails were pounded, the last breath was exhaled, and the sword had pierced the side, the crowds changed again. Gone were the ones seeking to draw the people into a murderous rage; their job was complete. All that was left were those who might have, at one time, cared about Jesus. Mingled with them were those who were curious, and others who had never lost their faith in Jesus. Now they turned away, "beating their breasts," and mourning the tragedy in which they had been complicit.

THE TWO THIEVES

> And with him they crucified two bandits, one on his right and one on his left. (Mark 15:27)

> One of the criminals who were hanged there kept deriding him and saying, "Are you not the Messiah? Save yourself and us!" But the other rebuked him, saying, "Do you not fear God, since you are under the same sentence of condemnation? And we indeed have been condemned justly, for we are getting what we deserve for our deeds, but this man has done nothing wrong." Then he said, "Jesus, remember me when you come into your kingdom." He replied, "Truly I tell you, today you will be with me in Paradise." (Luke 23:39–43)

It is not unusual for people to claim their innocence of the crimes that sent them to prison. Some hold to their stories for decades, and others right to the point of execution. It is sometimes observed that every person in prison is, by personal declaration, innocent of any crime. There are not many stories, however, of prisoners insisting on the innocence of their fellow inmates.

All four Gospel writers make reference to Jesus' two companions on Golgotha. Matthew, Mark, and Luke refer to them as "bandits," while John just describes them as "two others" (John 19:18). Matthew and

---

10. Psychologists call this "deindividuation." See http://www.psychology-lexicon.com/cms/glossary/glossary-d/deindividuation.html, accessed November 13, 2011.

The Sons of Abraham

Mark include the bandits among those who taunt Jesus as he dies (Matt 27:44, Mark 15:32). Only Luke offers an expanded and intimate version of the story.

The first man does not appear to be seeking redemption. As the other Gospel writers point out, the bandits were initially included in the company of those taunting Jesus as he suffered. Clearly if anyone, having been crucified on a Roman cross, were to be granted one wish, it would be to get off that tree of death. That is what the first man desires, and he makes his hopeless demand known to Jesus. In doing so, he knows that the whole request is a joke. If Jesus were truly God's anointed, he would not be on the cross in the first place, and even if he did slip up and get crucified, surely a true Messiah would have the wherewithal to make a dramatic escape and take a few other sufferers with him. In his agony, however, the man spits out his words as bitter sarcasm, knowing that all is lost. All he sees before him is another hapless Jew who ran afoul of the people with all the power.

Something is different with the other man. He recognizes something that the other ignores: Their guilt. They had committed crimes and were suffering the consequences, while Jesus came to the cross as an innocent man. This one slowly dying next to Jesus seems to know something about him, something more than that he had simply made the claim that he was Israel's Messiah. The man speaks of Jesus' innocence as though he has some familiarity with his life. He uses the language of "kingdom" in a way that suggests he might have heard Jesus speak at some point about God's reign. Could it be that he had been part of the curious crowds at some point in Jesus' ministry? Since his only appearance in the accounts of the Gospels is at the scene of the crucifixion, we can only speculate as to the source of his knowledge.

Execution on a cross was evidence of a Messiah's failure.[11] The first man seemed to understand that, and joined the living in their mockery of Jesus. The other man, however, allowed himself to challenge the belief that a crucified Messiah was a failed Messiah. Perhaps his life of living outside

---

11. "Crucifixion meant that the kingdom hadn't come, not that it had. Crucifixion of a would-be Messiah meant that he wasn't the Messiah, not that he was. When Jesus was crucified, every single disciple knew what it meant: we backed the wrong horse. The game is over. Whatever their expectations, and however Jesus had been trying to redefine those expectations, as far as they were concerned hope had crumbled into ashes." Wright, *Surprised by Hope*, 40.

the bounds of the law resulted in a willingness to consider possibilities that moved beyond what the authorities required. Criminals are generally good at figuring out a life that violates the rules of respectable society.

Scholars have long speculated about the nature of the two men's criminality. Could the two have been part of the band of Jewish Zealots who sought to overthrow Rome by violence? Most likely not, since the second man confesses to their deservedness when it comes to punishment. The Zealots would have likely seen themselves as justified in their actions rather than guilty of crimes.[12] As part of the local underworld, however, it is likely that these two thieves found themselves in easy company with the local Zealots. Perhaps the second man saw in Jesus a deeper resolve to obedience to God than he had seen in any of those who hoped to force God's hand. Regardless of the source of his information, the man clearly expected that Jesus' story was not over.

"Truly I tell you, today you will be with me in Paradise." These are strange words to be spoken at a time such as this. The hearer is dying—deservedly, by his own admission—and has asked only that Jesus remember him. Jesus offers a promise to be fulfilled on the other side of suffering and death, creating an image that stands in stark contrast to the man's present experience. The words are gracious, hopeful, and redeeming.

And, in accordance with the traditions of the day, completely and utterly wrong.

The text in Luke does not tell us whether the thief was sincere in his request to Jesus, or if he was making a compassionate attempt at humoring Jesus in his apparent delusion as the Messiah. Dorothy Sayers, in her play *The Man Born to Be King*, puts these words in the mouth of the thief:

> He's loony, that's all. Let 'im think he's Goddamighty, if it makes him feel any better . . . You're all right mate, ain't you? Of course you are. This 'ere's just a bad dream. One o' these days you'll come out in a cloud of glory and astonish them all. . . . There! he's smiling. He likes being talked to that way. . . . *(In a deeply respectful tone, humoring this harmless lunacy)* Sir, you'll remember me, won't you, when you come into your kingdom?[13]

---

12. John Nolland observes: "The logic of the second criminal's rebuke of the first is built upon the *first* deserving his fate, but the relevant statement comes in the plural to indicate that the second criminal is not distancing himself from his companion in this respect. Zealot 'freedom fighters' could hardly utter or agree with such a statement." Nolland, *Luke 18:35—24:53*, 1151.

13. Quoted in Neuhaus, *Death on a Friday Afternoon*, 37.

The Sons of Abraham

We cannot know for sure whether the thief was sincere or not; after all, both Matthew and Mark claim that both thieves were involved in the taunting of Jesus. I suspect, however, that Luke relayed the story because the request was, indeed, sincere even though it might have been a bit muddled. Luke makes it clear that it was the first thief who "derided" Jesus, not the second one. Even the framing of the request, calling to "Jesus" rather than to *Lord* or some other formal moniker suggests an intimate sense of solidarity that the man had with Jesus in their shared suffering and dying. Regardless, Jesus' words would have caught him up short for two reasons: First, because Jesus took him seriously and invited him to the last place the man expected; and, second, because people like the thief were not supposed to be eligible for entrance into *paradise*. In first-century Jewish thought, the image of paradise was that of a garden—perhaps a return to the original garden paradise of God's intention in Genesis 1 and 2—where people would rest as they awaited the day of resurrection. Not all people who died, however, were eligible for paradise; only those whose lives were sufficiently righteous would enjoy that post-life time of rest.[14]

Clearly, the thief did not qualify as a righteous person. And yet, Jesus promised him paradise.

The first thief dismissed Jesus as a hopeless failure who, along with his criminal companions, would die on that day. The other, however, would have seen something very different in the death of Jesus. He had not come to believe in a theology of salvation that hinged on Jesus' death, nor was evidence provided in the text that he prayed a prayer of repentance and trusted in Jesus with any kind of theological correctness. Yes, he believed in Jesus, but he would only have been able to believe in the one bruised, bleeding, and dying on the cross next to his. He only asked to be remembered, and Jesus, in his suffering and pain, welcomed the man to join him that day in paradise.

---

14. "In Jewish thought of Jesus' day, the imagery of 'paradise' was developed, using an old Persian term, out of reflection about the garden of Eden. . . . Paradise came to be understood as the pleasant resting place of some of the privileged dead prior to the great day of resurrection. After death, Jesus would certainly have been expected to be one of those who would go on to paradise. What is striking here is that the criminal who sues for mercy will be there with him " Nolland, *Luke 18:35—24:53*, 1153. See also Wright, *Surprised by Hope*, 150.

THE PILGRIMS AT PENTECOST

> Now there were devout Jews from every nation under heaven living in Jerusalem. And at this sound the crowd gathered and was bewildered, because each one heard them speaking in the native language of each. Amazed and astonished, they asked, "Are not all these who are speaking Galileans? And how is it that we hear, each of us, in our own native language? Parthians, Medes, Elamites, and residents of Mesopotamia, Judea and Cappadocia, Pontus and Asia, Phrygia and Pamphylia, Egypt and the parts of Libya belonging to Cyrene, and visitors from Rome, both Jews and proselytes, Cretans and Arabs—in our own languages we hear them speaking about God's deeds of power." (Acts 2:5–11)
>
> "Therefore let the entire house of Israel know with certainty that God has made him both Lord and Messiah, this Jesus whom you crucified."
>
> Now when they heard this, they were cut to the heart and said to Peter and to the other apostles, "Brothers, what should we do?" (Acts 2:36–37)

~

Like many extended families, Israel had periodic family reunions. The Day of Pentecost was a significant reunion time, held fifty days (the word Pentecost means *fiftieth*) after the observance of Passover. It was primarily a harvest festival and attendance was considered almost compulsory for devout Jews. So they came from the various nations where they had been scattered over the years.

The dispersion of the Jews (the *diaspora*, a Greek word meaning *sowing* or *scattering*) had taken place over many years. Some were scattered to surrounding nations because of business or work concerns; others were the descendants of those who had been exiled generations earlier. Regardless of the reasons for their scattering, the faithful Jews gathered in Jerusalem for the feast of Pentecost considered themselves citizens of foreign nations. The languages that were now primary for them were the languages of those nations.

Some might have been camping out in Jerusalem since Passover. Others would have come in stages as the obligations of home and commerce would allow. How many had been part of the rabble witnessing

The Sons of Abraham

and even affirming the crucifixion of Jesus we do not know. It appears, however, that Peter implicated them all in Jesus' death, even those who had not been present during that time. If they were faithful Jews, then it was assumed that they were guilty by association. All who were gathered that day were representatives of the nation of Israel—a people now being accused of murdering their own God-sent Messiah.

We are told in the opening words of Acts chapter 2 that

> . . . suddenly from heaven there came a sound like the rush of a violent wind, and it filled the entire house where they were sitting. Divided tongues, as of fire, appeared among them, and a tongue rested on each of them. All of them were filled with the Holy Spirit and began to speak in other languages, as the Spirit gave them ability. (Acts 2:2–4)

The pilgrims turned their attention to Peter and the others when ". . . at this sound the crowd gathered and was bewildered, because each one heard them speaking in the native language of each" (Acts 2:6). It is not clear whether or not they observed the appearance of the "tongues of fire" over the disciples' heads or if that phenomenon was limited to the upper room. Regardless, the people took notice.

First-century Jews would have been open to signs from God. Even beyond the commotion created by the sound of wind, seeing and hearing a band of peasant fishermen from Galilee suddenly becoming multilingual and proclaiming the great deeds of God would have the ring of authenticity. These acts were not religious parlor tricks designed to dazzle the masses; they would have been interpreted as signs that pointed to the glory of God.

It was, however, Peter's message that struck a chord with the people.[15] He pointed back to their own Scriptures by quoting from the prophet Joel and showing how the pouring out of the Holy Spirit was part of the long-term intention of God. While he declared their culpability in the unjust death of Jesus, Peter also proclaimed the reality of the resurrection and showed that death cannot have the upper hand because of what God has intended.

Imagine that you have made a difficult but exciting journey with family and friends to Jerusalem for the annual feast of Pentecost. The trip might have been long and arduous, but there would be great anticipation

---

15. Very likely delivered in Greek, the common language of the Roman Empire.

as you approached the city and set up camp, looking for relatives and friends you have not seen for at least a year. The sense of solidarity and unity would be palpable and you would be glad to be a part of this ancient family that traced its roots to the great patriarch Abraham. You would look forward to feasts and celebrations, prayer and remembrance. Your children might be working to memorize the Decalogue—the Ten Commandments—in order to participate in group recitations of the Law given by God to Moses at Mount Sinai.

Now, however, you are witnessing startling things and hearing a message that accuses everyone of the murder of the long-awaited Messiah—the One who would rescue Israel from her enemies. No one actually sees the resurrected Jesus on that day, but the witness of Peter and the others is compelling, and you and your family are "cut to the heart (v. 37)." What started out as a joyous family holiday has now collapsed into a national calamity. Perhaps you would be sorrowful yet expectant that God was acting again in the life of Israel; you also might be angry that these Galileans have wrecked everything.

If you have ever had your hopes and expectations for a holiday gathering dashed to bits, then you can imagine what the people felt. When I was ten years old, our family dog gave birth to a litter of puppies. My parents sold all but one of the pups, allowing me to keep one that would grow up in our house with its mother. On Christmas Eve morning that year, the dogs were romping in our kitchen and the pup took a fall, hitting the back of its head on the hard floor. It immediately went into convulsions and died at the vet's office later in the day. For me, Christmas—clearly my favorite childhood holiday—was destroyed that year. Unlike the pilgrims at Pentecost, there was not, for me, the possibility of a response that offered hope. It was just a time of sorrow that could only be healed over time.

Peter cast the responsibility for Jesus' death on all of Israel, both locally and globally. While Rome was seen as the vehicle for the crucifixion ("by the hands of those outside the law"), it was Israel that engineered this death. Peter's speech, however, moved quickly from the crucifixion to the resurrection and the outpouring of the Holy Spirit. The reader is not given reasons for Jesus' death (except that it was somehow in accordance with God's plan and foreknowledge[16]) but instead is shown a picture of

---

16. Some would say that *plan* and *foreknowledge* means that the entire drama of Jesus' life and death was perfectly orchestrated and predetermined by God. However, Peter's acknowledgement of God's role in the process still implicates the Jewish people and the

The Sons of Abraham

repentance and new life. The gathered pilgrims were called to repentance, and in so doing they were turning to God's Spirit, which was about to be generously poured out to them. According to this text, that is exactly what happened.[17]

Thousands of Jewish pilgrims believed Peter's testimony about Jesus, were overwhelmed by the Holy Spirit, and returned back to their homes among the nations. Days earlier, some of them might have been part of the mob that cried out for Jesus' death.

"His blood be on us and on our children!" (Matt 27:25)

The cry for blood-guilt would end, not in God's vengeance, but rather in reconciliation and the gift of the Holy Spirit. The image of Jesus' blood on the lives of the Jewish people turned from tragedy to the carrying of the very life of God's Messiah into the world, like seed pods scattered in the wind.

As they traveled home again, would the words of God, chronicled in the Torah, echo in their minds?

". . . and in you all the families of the earth shall be blessed." (Gen 12:3b)

Romans in the killing of Jesus, and calls for repentance—something that would seem unnecessary if they were simply acting in accordance with God's plan. I would suggest that *plan* is more consistent with God's ongoing plan to reconcile the world to himself (woven through the entire narrative of Scripture); *foreknowledge* recognizes that God sees what is coming long before anyone else does and knows how present events will culminate in the future. As John Sanders states: "The way of providence in the life of Jesus did not occur by some predetermined plan. Everything is not being worked out according to some eternal script. God responds to his creatures and gets involved in the give and take of life. God remained faithful to his original commitment while working to fulfill it in ways the covenant people did not anticipate." Sanders, *The God Who Risks: A Theology of Providence*, 137.

17. McKnight comments on this text: ". . . Telling the Story of Jesus is anointed by God to awaken sin in the person who hears the Story of Jesus. Instead of focusing on their sin, though Peter does lay blame on them for crucifying Jesus or implicates them in that dreadful deed, Peter focuses on Jesus, and the Jesus Story awakens a consciousness of sin and a need for Jesus to be their Messiah, Lord, and Savior." McKnight, *The King Jesus Gospel*, 145.

Atonement at Ground Zero

GAMALIEL

> When they had brought them, they had them stand before the council. The high priest questioned them, saying, "We gave you strict orders not to teach in this name, yet here you have filled Jerusalem with your teaching and you are determined to bring this man's blood on us." But Peter and the apostles answered, "We must obey God rather than any human authority. The God of our ancestors raised up Jesus, whom you had killed by hanging him on a tree. God exalted him at his right hand as Leader and Savior, so that he might give repentance to Israel and forgiveness of sins. And we are witnesses to these things, and so is the Holy Spirit whom God has given to those who obey him."
>
> When they heard this, they were enraged and wanted to kill them. But a Pharisee in the council named Gamaliel, a teacher of the law, respected by all the people, stood up and ordered the men to be put outside for a short time. Then he said to them, "Fellow-Israelites, consider carefully what you propose to do to these men. For some time ago Theudas rose up, claiming to be somebody, and a number of men, about four hundred, joined him; but he was killed, and all who followed him were dispersed and disappeared. After him Judas the Galilean rose up at the time of the census and got people to follow him; he also perished, and all who followed him were scattered. So in the present case, I tell you, keep away from these men and let them alone; because if this plan or this undertaking is of human origin, it will fail; but if it is of God, you will not be able to overthrow them—in that case you may even be found fighting against God!" (Acts 5:27–39)

Throughout the book of Acts it is clear that following Jesus was a risky vocation. Persecution and murder came right on the heels of the remarkable events of Acts 2, yet the early adopters of this new movement continued to multiply and extend their reach. At this stage of the story, these first followers would have seen their new life in Jesus as a renewal of the faith of their ancestors—a distinctively Jewish story. Their own religious leaders, however, took exception to what was happening. The reports of miraculous healings and the proclamation that Israel's Messiah had come flew in the face of the status quo. Dealing with such tension was more than the leaders could take.

The theory of cognitive dissonance describes the tension that is created when new ideas or beliefs conflict with those formerly held. For example, some years ago I received a phone call from a man who was in college with me twenty years earlier. He shared with me his belief that I married a particular young woman and then later divorced. I explained to him that I did not marry that woman, but had been happily married for many years to a completely different woman. The man argued with me because I had just created tension for him, offering a narrative of my life that conflicted with his own understanding. He ended the call with a significant level of frustration and disbelief.

According to the theory of cognitive dissonance, there are basically three ways to eliminate this tension. The first is to deny the validity of the new ideas; the second is to shore up the old ideas with information that diminishes the power of the new ideas; the third is to change the nature of the new ideas so that they become compatible with the old ideas.[18] According to Acts 5, there is a fourth way that is a variation on the first: Demand the purveyors of the new ideas to become silent upon the threat of death.[19]

The members of the Sanhedrin were worked up to the point of mob violence when they found Peter and his friends continuing to speak about Jesus after they mysteriously escaped from prison. It seems that the only action they could think of to resolve the tension of the situation was murder—the ultimate action that seeks to invalidate competing ideas. It was Gamaliel who stopped the violence and brought some form of perspective to the people.

Gamaliel doesn't receive a lot of attention in the New Testament. Jewish tradition describes him as a devoted Pharisee his entire life; some Christian traditions claim that he was not only the apostle Paul's mentor, but that he also became a subversive Christian, remaining a member of the Sanhedrin in order to calm the storms of persecution when they arose. Regardless of his true history, Gamaliel is shown in Scripture as

---

18. Leon Fetsinger's webpage offers a helpful and entertaining summary of the theory of cognitive dissonance: http://tip.psychology.org/festinge.html

19. This pattern has recurred throughout church history, including the Church's demand that Galileo quit defending Copernicus's theory of heliocentrism (identifying the sun as the center of the universe rather than the earth). When he refused, he was placed in house arrest until the day of his death. Today, denouncements on the Internet and removal from scholarly societies are the preferred responses to theological cognitive dissonance.

one who brings another prophetic voice to the events of Christianity's ground zero.

Gamaliel's point is well taken: Jesus was not the first so-called Messiah to arrive on the scene. There were others before him, and there would be others after him. None came to anything, and everyone involved met a dismal fate. True, Jesus died a criminal's death; that alone should have closed the book on his messianic fantasy. The claims and actions of his followers, however, were different from others. Rather than being scattered, they risked their lives by continuing to proclaim that God had raised Jesus from the dead, that God's Spirit had exploded upon the earth, and that the signs and wonders in which they participated were evidence of this new reality. Gamaliel's counsel to his colleagues was to step back and let it go; if this drama was like the others, then it would meet a similar, self-destructive fate. If, however, what these sketchy characters claimed was true, then the leaders of Israel could find themselves battling their own God. Gamaliel's influence was such that the members of the council took his direction, but not before administering a good flogging to the culprits.

Gamaliel and Caiaphas had something in common: Both gave statements that were prophetic in nature, intentionally or otherwise. There was an important difference: Caiaphas laid the groundwork for false accusation and murder; Gamaliel called for theological perspective and the possibility that God could truly be at work.

In his statement, Gamaliel offers a fifth response to resolving cognitive dissonance: Consider that the old ideas are misplaced, and the new ones are worth considering. For some, that would open up a new possibility for life; for others, such an option would be unthinkable.

7

The Occupying Forces

PONTIUS PILATE

> Then they took Jesus from Caiaphas to Pilate's headquarters. It was early in the morning. They themselves did not enter the headquarters, so as to avoid ritual defilement and to be able to eat the Passover. So Pilate went out to them and said, "What accusation do you bring against this man?" They answered, "If this man were not a criminal, we would not have handed him over to you." Pilate said to them, "Take him yourselves and judge him according to your law." The Jews replied, "We are not permitted to put anyone to death." (This was to fulfill what Jesus had said when he indicated the kind of death he was to die.) Then Pilate entered the headquarters again, summoned Jesus, and asked him, "Are you the King of the Jews?" Jesus answered, "Do you ask this on your own, or did others tell you about me?" Pilate replied, "I am not a Jew, am I? Your own nation and the chief priests have handed you over to me. What have you done?" Jesus answered, "My kingdom is not from this world. If my kingdom were from this world, my followers would be fighting to keep me from being handed over to the Jews. But as it is, my kingdom is not from here." Pilate asked him, "So you are a king?" Jesus answered, "You say that I am a king. For this I was born, and for this I came into the world, to testify to the truth. Everyone who belongs to the truth listens to my voice." Pilate asked him, "What is truth?" (John 18:28–38)

⁓

THE GREAT ITALIAN POET Dante Alighieri strategically places some shadowy figures just inside the gates of Hell in canto three of his brilliant work,

The Divine Comedy. There is some speculation as to the identity of these smoky figures in the dark, but one likely candidate is Pontius Pilate. It could be appropriate that he stands just inside the gate but not fully in the depths of Hell itself, since he was the prince of vacillation in the drama that ended with Jesus' sentence of death.

Outside of the New Testament, not a great deal is known about Pilate. He is portrayed there as a political chameleon, dismissing the Jewish leaders one minute—"I find no basis for an accusation against this man" (Luke 23:4)—and then caving into their demands when he is cornered with the allegiances of his own empire as the Jewish leaders scream, "If you release this man, you are no friend of the emperor. Everyone who claims to be a king sets himself against the emperor" (John 19:12).

Matthew, Mark, and Luke offer similar accounts of Pilate's interaction with Jesus. His challenges to Jesus are brief and to the point, resulting in a swift death sentence. In Matthew's telling of the story, however, Pilate's wife makes an appearance. She warns her husband to steer clear of Jesus, not because he is dangerous, but because he is innocent:

> "Have nothing to do with that innocent man, for today I have suffered a great deal because of a dream about him." (Matthew 27:19)

How she suffered remains a mystery. But she was convinced of Jesus' innocence and perhaps feared that her husband's involvement in the schemes of the Jewish leaders would lead to something disastrous. Pilate himself saw that the accusations were a sham, that the Jewish leaders had their own issues when it came to Jesus.

> For he realized that it was out of jealousy that they had handed him over. (Matthew 27:18)

It is in John's account where Pilate's distress is dramatically portrayed. After he holds the initial audience with the Jewish leaders, Pilate tries to engage Jesus in conversation. Jesus won't respond on Pilate's terms, but offers what must have been puzzling, mystical answers to the governor's questions. Even when Pilate throws out a philosophical challenge—"What is truth?" (John 18:38)—Jesus remains silent. He offers no defense, but only strange statements about the nature of his kingdom.[1]

---

1. In the apocryphal *Acts of Pilate*, written between the second and fourth centuries, Jesus and Pilate carry the conversation a little further: "Jesus says to him: Truth is from heaven. Pilate says: Is truth not upon earth? Jesus says to Pilate: Thou seest how those

The Occupying Forces

Pilate did not need to wrestle with this problem. In his position he could have easily agreed to the execution of a peasant in order to keep the peace. What was one scrawny Jew when his own reputation as a mid-level ruler might be at stake? Commanding swift judgment would shore up his position of power in the eyes of the people and no one would question his decision.

But Pilate did wrestle. His wife's dream must have touched his own misgivings about condemning this man Jesus. That Pilate would spend time talking with Jesus suggests that he had more interest in him than merely as a bothersome rebel. When the cry for the release of Barabbas filled the air, Pilate must have been dumbstruck, even though he was the one who suggested the criminal's release (Matt. 27:17). Surely he expected the people to see the folly in the suggestion and come to their senses. Exchange a common thief for a wandering preacher—one worth a conversation with a Roman governor? They couldn't be serious.

The people *were* serious. And finally, Pilate crumbled.

I wonder if Pilate ever made his way to Golgotha to see how things were going. Did he ever look upon the man he had condemned? In the night, perhaps he lay awake, suffering as his wife had suffered in her dreams. Even though he made a show of absolving himself by a ceremonial hand-washing in front of the crowd (Matt 27:24), it is unlikely that the mental torment would evaporate any time soon.

For Pilate, in spite of the personal struggles he had regarding Jesus, this was ultimately an issue of power.

> "Do you not know that I have power to release you, and power to crucify you?" Jesus answered him, "You would have no power over me unless it had been given you from above." (John 19:10–11)

Pilate may have interpreted Jesus' words as a reference to the Emperor, from whom Pilate had received his appointment as governor of Judea. Certainly Caesar was "above" Pilate in the empire's political food chain. Jesus, however, was continuing to speak of the kingdom of God. This authority from *above* was the source of the same new birth that Jesus had informed Nicodemus must come from *above*.[2] Yes, on this day

---

who speak the truth are judged by those that have the power upon earth." James, *The Gospel of Nicodemus, or The Acts of Pilate*, III/2.

2. The Greek of the New Testament uses the same word for *above* in John 3:3, 7 and John 19:11.

the power of Rome would have its way with Jesus. Pilate and Jesus both knew this, but viewed that power through different lenses. In the death of Jesus, Rome would unleash its power and stand dominant in the world they had conquered. There would also be a new alliance between former enemies who constantly jockeyed for position in this backwater region called Israel.

> That same day Herod and Pilate became friends with each other; before this they had been enemies. (Luke 23:12)

Both Herod and Pilate were representatives of the powers that dominated Israel. Both were skilled at eliminating rebels and pretenders to their thrones. Although they shared some level of interest in and admiration of Jesus, putting him to death was in line with actions that they had taken in the past. With Jesus gone, as unnecessary as his death might have seemed to these two rulers, their respective strength and new friendship would remind the world that their power was unshakable.

Or so they thought.

THE EXECUTIONERS

> Then the soldiers of the governor took Jesus into the governor's headquarters, and they gathered the whole cohort around him. They stripped him and put a scarlet robe on him, and after twisting some thorns into a crown, they put it on his head. They put a reed in his right hand and knelt before him and mocked him, saying, "Hail, King of the Jews!" They spat on him, and took the reed and struck him on the head. After mocking him, they stripped him of the robe and put his own clothes on him. Then they led him away to crucify him. (Matt 27:27–31)

Modern executions in the western world have a clinical quality to them. The day and time are set, the witnesses are scheduled, and the process is prepared. As the condemned person stands ready, a death warrant is read, last words are spoken, and the sentence is carried out swiftly and, many would hope, relatively pain free. There is no creative freedom for the executioner. The work is prescribed with focus and precision. No matter the suffering inflicted upon the victims by the condemned person, the retributive death will, in places like the United States, be painless and quick.

Not so in the ancient world. The work of execution had an artistic element to it. The drama of William Wallace's execution portrayed in the film *Braveheart* has some historical precedent. Ancient executions were public and symbolic, the participants sometimes treated as actors in a play. At times the executioners were free to take their time and be creative in the process of extinguishing a human life. In first-century Palestine, executions of non-Roman citizens might be brutal and agonizing, but they were crafted with intention, skill, and even a little artistic freedom.

Jesus' executioners seemed to enjoy their freedom to torture and kill. Whether out of sadistic inclinations or sheer boredom, these men relished their work. A full cohort of soldiers, possibly numbering eight hundred men, surrounded Jesus and began their games. Luke has Herod as the provider of the robe that Jesus wore; Matthew and Luke assign that gift of adornment to the Roman soldiers. Either way, it was a sign of mockery and the men enjoyed using it as a tool for their amusement. There would be no king except Caesar, and this ridiculous pretender to the throne—Jewish or Roman—was good for nothing more than the sport of the troops.

There is only one account of Jesus directly impacting the life of a Roman soldier. In Luke's account it happens indirectly, through a messenger, but Matthew relays the story in a more personal way, with the centurion approaching Jesus face to face.

> When he entered Capernaum, a centurion came to him, appealing to him and saying, "Lord, my servant is lying at home paralyzed, in terrible distress." And he said to him, "I will come and cure him." The centurion answered, "Lord, I am not worthy to have you come under my roof; but only speak the word, and my servant will be healed. For I also am a man under authority, with soldiers under me; and I say to one, 'Go', and he goes, and to another, 'Come', and he comes, and to my slave, 'Do this', and the slave does it." When Jesus heard him, he was amazed and said to those who followed him, "Truly I tell you, in no one in Israel have I found such faith. I tell you, many will come from east and west and will eat with Abraham and Isaac and Jacob in the kingdom of heaven, while the heirs of the kingdom will be thrown into the outer darkness, where there will be weeping and gnashing of teeth." And to the

> centurion Jesus said, "Go; let it be done for you according to your faith." And the servant was healed in that hour. (Matt 8:5–13)

Word of this miraculous act of mercy would have found its way to some of the Roman troops. There must have been some standing in the cohort on the day of Jesus' crucifixion who had been impacted by the stories of his works or those who had loved ones who had been touched by him. It is likely that the centurion in Matthew's account was present on that awful day, unable to exert sufficient authority upward toward the governor in order to stop the torture. He might, however, have ordered restraint to the 80–100 soldiers under his own command. He understood that he was a man under authority.

The soldiers who facilitated the crucifixions on that day behaved in a contradictory manner when it came to Jesus. There is at one moment brutality; at the next there seems to be something akin to care and reverence. The executioners had been given their orders and there would be no negotiation or hesitation on their part. At the same time, their deadly precision was interrupted by something that could be wonder or awe.

People who were crucified suffered in numerous ways, including the endurance of the pain of intense thirst. There would not be relief offered for the agony inflicted on the limbs of the victim or an easing of the pressure on the lungs as the weight of the body constricted the ability to breathe. Why satisfy the dying person's thirst during the deathwatch? Yet, when Jesus cried out his need for drink, he was given the cheap wine that the soldiers used to refresh themselves while they worked. It is only John who records this action:

> After this, when Jesus knew that all was now finished, he said (in order to fulfill the Scripture), "I am thirsty." A jar full of sour wine was standing there. So they put a sponge full of the wine on a branch of hyssop and held it to his mouth. When Jesus had received the wine, he said, "It is finished." Then he bowed his head and gave up his spirit." (John 19:28–30)

Jesus, who shared the cup of wine with his friends just hours earlier in preparation for his impending crucifixion, received a final taste of wine that ushered him through the doorway of death. In an ironic twist to the story, Jesus' executioners serve him in a reversal of how he had served his friends. It is possible that his followers who were witnessing Jesus' death

The Occupying Forces

recalled at that moment his puzzling words when he had cautioned James and John about seeking positions of power:

> "You do not know what you are asking. Are you able to drink the cup that I drink . . .? (Mark 10:38a)

A taste of wine that was shared by friends as a mere representation of death now marries the symbol with the reality. Jesus drinks, and then he dies.

In order to avoid religious offense, the Jewish leaders convinced Pilate to hasten the death of the condemned men by breaking their legs—after all, what were three human lives compared to the preserving of religious sensibilities? This action would prohibit the dying men from relieving the suffocating pressure on their lungs when they could no longer push themselves upward from the braces where their feet rested on the crosses. Pilate granted the permission, and the soldiers obediently responded. However, when they approached Jesus, truncheons in hand, they hesitated. They believed that he had already died, and another action was taken:

> Then the soldiers came and broke the legs of the first and of the other who had been crucified with him. But when they came to Jesus and saw that he was already dead, they did not break his legs. Instead, one of the soldiers pierced his side with a spear, and at once blood and water came out. (John 19:32–34)

Crushing Jesus' legs along with those of the other dying men would make sense. All would be dead soon anyway, so why bother with the piercing of the side? John claims that it is in keeping with the fulfillment of Scripture:

> These things occurred so that the Scripture might be fulfilled, "None of his bones shall be broken." And again another passage of Scripture says, "They will look on the one whom they have pierced." (John 19:36–37)[3]

Imagine the soldiers looking up at the limp body of Jesus, hanging skeletally on the cross. They wait, gazing up at him, and find it unnecessary

---

3. Some might say that the entire scene was scripted by God as part of his overall plan of redemption. Others would say that the prophets of old saw how the dominant culture would respond to God's anointed one long before the events took place. Either way, the Scripture is fulfilled.

(even objectionable!) to smash his bones. Instead, they perform a precise surgical act designed to determine death. As blood and water flow, separated from each other by the ceasing of the body's vital functions, death is certified by the experts. Again, it seems like a reverent act offered by those whose vocations were not typically characterized by reverence.

On that day, Jesus died for two reasons: First, death is the inevitable end for all who live; and second, a death suffered in brutality came to all who faced off with the dominant powers of the day, both political and also religious. When one claims a lordship that stands over and against the powers that control the human stories of everyday life, harsh action will be taken.

After cleaning themselves up and returning to their barracks, the soldiers' conversation would probably run as it always did after such a task as this was completed. Today, however, there would be new things to consider: The death of an obviously innocent man, the unusual rage of the crowds against him, and the softness seen in certain officers that was out of character for men hardened by war and mass executions. The talk about this day of death would be like no other.

The soldiers might have joked about the thorny branches they had woven together and pressed into the skin on Jesus' head. A king should have a crown, and a parody of the king should have a comic crown. A rack of thorns shoved onto the head would remind a failed king of the crown he had desired and mock him as he died in the knowledge that a gold crown would never be his. Others could have laughed at the irony displayed by the crown of thorns because it also parodied the victor's laurel wreath that was granted to those being honored after a military success. It was only fitting that a failed king should wear a wreath of pain and suffering rather than one of honor and glory.

It would be hard for these men to imagine that this dying, shamed Messiah somehow represented victory to those who continued to follow him. Overall, the soldiers merely did their jobs. In the end, it would be just another day when one more of many dusty peasants would be hanged out to die. There was one soldier, however, who recognized that it was not just another day and that this particular dusty peasant was different from the rest.

THE CENTURION AT GOLGOTHA

> Now when the centurion, who stood facing him, saw that in this way he breathed his last, he said, "Truly this man was God's Son!" (Mark 15:39)

∼

The Romans had many gods, and these gods were not shy about procreating in the most human of ways. The Greek and Roman pantheons were filled with gods, goddesses, and their offspring—sons and daughters of the gods. Like their human subjects, the ancient divines were products of unskilled labor, so to speak.

Jupiter (and his Greek equivalent, Zeus[4]) was chief of all the Roman gods. Through his incestuous marriage to his sister Juno, the god Mars was produced. Mars was the god of war, considered the father of the Roman people, and was the preferred god of the Roman legions. Mars, as a son of a god, was of great value in Roman culture, particularly to those in military service.

Jews, as monotheists—believing only in the God of Abraham, Isaac, and Jacob—also had a way of thinking about the title, Son of God. Rather than reducing sonship to divine procreation, as the Romans had, first-century Jews would hear that term as a reference to the people of God—Israel—and to her anticipated representative, the messianic king who would come one day.[5] Their ancestors would identify the Davidic throne with the title of divine sonship, as proclaimed in the Psalm of David in response to the conspiring of the nations against Israel:

> He who sits in the heavens laughs; the Lord has them in derision. Then he will speak to them in his wrath, and terrify them in his fury, saying, "I have set my king on Zion, my holy hill." I will tell of the decree of the Lord: He said to me, "You are my son; today I have begotten you. Ask of me, and I will make the nations your heritage, and the ends of the earth your possession" (Ps 2:4–8).[6]

---

4. Zeus was the one who threw lightning bolts at his enemies. This kind of action is often attributed to the God of the Bible, but throwing lightning was clearly a Greco-Roman preference for their gods.

5. "... In the first century the regular Jewish meaning of this title had nothing to do with an incipient trinitarianism; it referred to the king as *Israel's representative*. Israel was the son of YHWH: the king who would come to take her destiny on himself would share this title." Wright, *Jesus and the Victory of God*, 485–6.

6. "'You are my son' (v.7) is the only appearance of 'son' as title of the Davidic king in

In Jesus' day, the term captured the full life and destiny of Israel, and called to mind the image of God's Messiah who would lead Israel back to the place of God's intention. It was a term rich with meaning and hope for Israel.

Given the difference in interpretations, it is interesting that Mark[7] would include the Centurion's words in his account of Jesus' death. There would be risks for both Jewish and Gentile readers as their ways of imaging "Son of God" would conflict with each other. The significance, however, might be found in the rightful declaration about Jesus being made, not by one of Jesus' own kinfolk, but by a pagan soldier. His paradigm for "Son of God" might not be clear, but the testimony was still correct.

It is not known whether or not this soldier was sympathetic to the Jewish community or familiar with their religious terminology. He could have been framing his perspective on Jesus in terms familiar to the Jews or in a way that drew Jesus into his Roman understanding of deity. Some speculate that this was the same centurion whose servant Jesus healed. We don't know that for sure, since the text doesn't offer that connection. Regardless, this was a leader of Roman soldiers, standing over the horrible crucifixion process, who offered one of the earliest confessions of faith: *Truly this man was God's Son!*

Matthew's account places the centurion within earshot when Jesus cried out one of the loneliest, most painful of human utterances:

> "Eli, Eli, lema sabachthani?" that is, "My God, my God, why have you forsaken me?" (Matt 27:46)

Watching this man die, the centurion would have wondered why a community of people would be intent on doing away with someone like Jesus. He would have been aware of Pilate's claim that there was no fault to be found in Jesus, and yet here was the man, dying alone and in agony. Perhaps hearing him utter words of forgiveness (not to mention experiencing the accompanying earthquake) would cause him to marvel at one who would die so nobly. If there really was a God, then he would have a son like this. No wonder Jesus cried out, grieving the absence of

---

the psalms. It is the ritual counterpart to the prophetic promise, 'I will be his father, and he shall be my son,' given to David in II Samuel 7:14." Mays, *Psalms*, 47.

7. Also Matthew (27:54). Luke quotes the centurion saying, "Certainly this man was innocent" (23:47).

his God, whether it was the God of Abraham or the mighty Jupiter who had his back turned.

The Jews, on the other hand, would have recognized Jesus' words as coming from a familiar text of their Scriptures:

> My God, my God, why have you forsaken me? Why are you so far from helping me, from the words of my groaning? O my God, I cry by day, but you do not answer; and by night, but find no rest. (Ps 22:1–2)

Yes, Jesus was alone and dying. He had claimed to be the Son of God, but his heavenly Father appeared to be disinterested in his Son's suffering and death. Indeed, he had been forsaken and everyone knew it.

Or was he? The words that Jesus quoted were words of pain and suffering, whether directly from King David or from the later people of Israel, a people in exile who were suffering under the boot heel of foreign invaders. The people watching Jesus die would know that they, too, were a people in pain and exile, left to the intentions of Rome to dictate a future that they thought was in the hands of God. In Jesus' mournful cry, he identified with the people before him, taking on the ultimate in forsakenness into his body, as the complicity of Rome and Jerusalem had their way with him. In his very being Jesus endured the power and rage of the force of evil, and he did it in complete identification with his people.

In the person of Jesus, God fully identified with his people in the totality of what it means to be human, and then allowed all the pain, suffering, and death that the world has to offer to have its way with him.[8] As Jesus died, he fully bore the name extended to him at his birth:

> ". . . and they shall name him Emmanuel", which means, "God is with us." (Matt 1:23)

The Centurion saw something that others had missed: This dying one, this Son of God, had been *with us*. He was with us all the time, and we killed him.

---

8. Goldingay acknowledges the Father's identification with the Son and, ultimately, with the world: "Understandings of the atonement sometimes infer (partly on the basis of speaking of God's abandonment) that the cross is a moment when Father and Son are separated, when God's face is turned away. There is indeed a sense in which the Father's face is turned away. In the sense in which the psalms use that expression, the turning away of God's face means that God does nothing. But in our own sense of the expression, there is no reason to reckon that this is so. Indeed, this is the moment when God is in Christ reconciling the world, and to that end the Father needs to be in association with the Son. The Father is watching as the Son suffers. The Father thus goes through a different form of suffering from the Son's, but one that is just as real and at least as painful." Goldingay, 837.

THE GUARDS AT THE TOMB

> While they were going, some of the guard went into the city and told the chief priests everything that had happened. After the priests had assembled with the elders, they devised a plan to give a large sum of money to the soldiers, telling them, "You must say, 'His disciples came by night and stole him away while we were asleep.' If this comes to the governor's ears, we will satisfy him and keep you out of trouble." So they took the money and did as they were directed. And this story is still told among the Jews to this day. (Matt 28:11–15)

~

The Tomb of the Unknowns at Arlington National Cemetery in Virginia is guarded by sentinels twenty-four hours a day. The highly structured requirements of the guards convey a deep sense of reverence and symbolism that recognizes the many soldiers who have died in battle but were never identified. The guards are monitored closely and can lose the privilege of serving in that capacity if they fail in keeping the required standards.

As with similar monuments in a variety of nations, the tomb encases the remains of an anonymous warrior that fell in battle while serving his nation. The body serves as an honorific symbol for all soldiers who died in the tragedy of war but were never given a proper burial. These unnamed, unrecognized dead were absorbed into the earth upon which they fell. The guards have no acquaintance with this fallen comrade of a long-ago war, yet they protect that tomb because the assignment has been given and the service is perceived as an act of honor.

The guarding of Jesus' tomb, however, came about not out of honor but rather through fear. This was not to be a guard that kept a memory alive; it was a guard sent to ensure that the memory would vanish from history. The Jewish leaders requested the guard from Pilate, concerned that the disciples would steal the body and claim that Jesus had risen from the dead (see Matt 27:62–66). They anticipated a disaster should that happen. After all, the only thing worse than a failed Messiah was a resurrected one. To have their public believe such a fabrication would mark the end of their doctrine of control. Their demand for a guard of Roman soldiers caused Pilate to comply without question:

The Occupying Forces

> "Therefore command that the tomb be made secure until the third day; otherwise his disciples may go and steal him away, and tell the people, 'He has been raised from the dead', and the last deception would be worse than the first." Pilate said to them, "You have a guard of soldiers; go, make it as secure as you can." So they went with the guard and made the tomb secure by sealing the stone. (Matt 27:64–66)

Whether the guards took their assignment seriously or not is a matter of speculation; the protection of the tomb of an executed Jewish peasant probably wasn't high on their list of key assignments. However, that their governor would demand such action would suggest that insurrection might be a concern—there were, after all, Jews who would love to see the Romans washed out of Israel in a river of their own blood. Even if the guards dismissed the talk of Jesus rising from the dead as religious superstition, they would have been on alert for those who would try to force the prophecy by their own devices.

Matthew tells us that the guards did indeed witness a disturbance of Jesus' grave, but not in the way they had expected. We are told that an earthquake shook the ground just after the two Marys arrived at the tomb and that an angel appeared, rolling the heavy stone away from the entrance. The guards did not seem to respond to this event like hardened Roman soldiers:

> For fear of him the guards shook and became like dead men. But the angel said to the women, "Do not be afraid . . ." (Matt 28:4–5)

The angel ignored the soldiers completely, leaving them to their terror, and turned his attention to the women, inviting them out of their fear into a place of trusting what God was doing. Once the women responded to the angel's instructions to communicate what had happened to the other disciples, the soldiers recovered from their shock sufficiently to report what had taken place. Interestingly, they did not go to their own military superiors; they went to the religious leaders, who immediately bribed the soldiers in order to buy their silence. The soldiers must have told, with some truthfulness, what they had seen. Had they lied and claimed that they had been overpowered by a band a Jews who had raided the tomb and stolen Jesus' body, then there would have been no need for their silence to be purchased.

The Bible bears witness to God's work, at particular times and places in history, in and through his people. The stories, prayers, words of wisdom, letters, and prophetic declarations all point to God and his mission in the world. The guards at the tomb would be witnesses of a different kind. Years later they might have confessed to their comrades that they saw strange, terrifying things during that night of sentry duty. Some might have written the experience off as a result of fatigue or the capricious teasings of some lesser god or goddess. Others, however, might have remembered something different. Perhaps, while assisting at later executions of some early Christians, one of the soldiers would have remembered that awful night and considered the connection between that experience and the death of ones who claimed allegiance to the Jesus of that cold tomb. Either way, such an encounter would not leave even the most stoic warrior unchanged.

At this point in the story, the tomb breaks open, the terrifying angel appears, and two sets of witnesses are dispatched. The women, addressed directly and comfortingly by the angel, are sent to the other disciples. Their testimony would erupt in hope, astonishment, and joy. The guards, shaken from their catatonia, escape with their lives to tell a similar story. This act of witness, however, would result in a cover-up and a denial of the experience; it would be good news for some, and bad news for others.

The apostle Paul understood this counter-dynamic of witness, and said it well:

> For we are the aroma of Christ to God among those who are being saved and among those who are perishing; to the one a fragrance from death to death, to the other a fragrance from life to life. (2 Cor. 2:15–16a)

For the faithful, the empty tomb would smell like the freshness of new life. For the others, it would only carry the stink of decay and the weight of fear that comes with the possibility that one's dominant story of control and certainty is about to be torn to shreds. The report of the guards revealed their recognition that this routine time of execution and burial was like no other they had experienced. For those receiving the report, it would no longer be the death that concerned them; it would be the unraveling of their preferred reality of control that would come with the insistence that in Jesus—the failed, crucified, cursed, would-be Messiah—there was new life.

8

Friends, Family, and Followers

THE MARYS

> When the soldiers had crucified Jesus, they took his clothes and divided them into four parts, one for each soldier. They also took his tunic; now the tunic was seamless, woven in one piece from the top. So they said to one another, "Let us not tear it, but cast lots for it to see who will get it." This was to fulfill what the Scripture says, "They divided my clothes among themselves, and for my clothing they cast lots." And that is what the soldiers did. Meanwhile, standing near the cross of Jesus were his mother, and his mother's sister, Mary the wife of Clopas, and Mary Magdalene. When Jesus saw his mother and the disciple whom he loved standing beside her, he said to his mother, "Woman, here is your son." Then he said to the disciple, "Here is your mother." And from that hour the disciple took her into his own home. (John 19:23–27)

THE CONTRAST BETWEEN THE callousness of the soldiers, who gambled away Jesus' garments, and the quiet, sorrowful faithfulness of the women is striking. The soldiers turned away from the dying Jesus and focused on taking ownership of his only earthly possession. It probably never occurred to the soldiers that by grasping this garment they were taking all, in a tangible sense, that Jesus had to give to them.

There is another account of someone grasping Jesus' garment in order to receive something:

> Now there was a woman who had been suffering from hemorrhages for twelve years. She had endured much under many physicians, and had spent all that she had; and she was no better, but rather grew worse. She had heard about Jesus, and came up behind him in the crowd and touched his cloak, for she said, "If I but touch his clothes, I will be made well." Immediately her hemorrhage stopped; and she felt in her body that she was healed of her disease. (Mark 5:25–29)

Like the soldiers at Jesus' crucifixion, this woman received all that Jesus had to give, but in a way that transcended any sense of material gain. It appears that this woman saw something in Jesus that many others had missed. To grasp at Jesus' cloak was not, for her, the act of a scavenger; it was a desperate touch that hoped for new life.

It seemed that the women who came in contact with Jesus often saw what others had missed. His mother, Mary, saw that faithfulness to the call of God surpassed social and religious expectations. Even though her pregnancy would be considered scandalous in her context, her obedience to God would result in holiness rather than in disgrace:

> The angel said to her, "Do not be afraid, Mary, for you have found favor with God. And now, you will conceive in your womb and bear a son, and you will name him Jesus. He will be great, and will be called the Son of the Most High, and the Lord God will give to him the throne of his ancestor David. He will reign over the house of Jacob for ever, and of his kingdom there will be no end." Mary said to the angel, "How can this be, since I am a virgin?" The angel said to her, "The Holy Spirit will come upon you, and the power of the Most High will overshadow you; therefore the child to be born will be holy; he will be called Son of God." (Luke 1:30–35)

A woman in Samaria, passed around from man to man like a plaything, recognized that Jesus was the one that her people were expecting to come—the Messiah:

> The woman said to him, "I know that Messiah is coming" (who is called Christ). "When he comes, he will proclaim all things to us." Jesus said to her, "I am he, the one who is speaking to you" . . . Many Samaritans from that city believed in him because of

the woman's testimony, "He told me everything I have ever done." (John 4:25–26, 39)

At Jesus' tomb, the women understood that Jesus was not only absent, but had been raised from the dead, and they were commissioned by an angel to report this unbelievable story to the men who had not yet seen:

> But the angel said to the women, "Do not be afraid; I know that you are looking for Jesus who was crucified. He is not here; for he has been raised, as he said. Come, see the place where he lay. Then go quickly and tell his disciples, 'He has been raised from the dead, and indeed he is going ahead of you to Galilee; there you will see him.' This is my message for you." (Matt 28:5–7)

Mother's Day in the US is a national observance of motherhood. It often involves elaborate cards, breakfast in bed, the promise of chores done, and the blessing of the mother's presence in the life of her family. It can be a warm time of gathering, but it also has become disconnected from its own origins. In the late nineteenth century, mothers of those who died in the American Civil War gathered to call for peace. No longer, they demanded, should their sons be slaughtered in battle. At its inception, Mother's Day was an anti-war movement.[1]

Just as Civil-War era women seemed to understand about and act upon the ravages of war, so did the women who surrounded Jesus seem to understand him at a level that was deeper than what others could comprehend. When confronted by the angel at the tomb, they were quick to believe the message of resurrection, and their hope turned to action as they raced to tell the others. In John's Gospel, it is Mary Magdalene who discovers the empty tomb, and she runs to tell Peter about her discovery. Peter and "the other disciple" (John 20:2) bolt to the tomb to see for themselves. They were not content to take Mary's word that Jesus was gone from the tomb. Most of us, like the two disciples, would have wanted to see for ourselves. It was the women, however, who were the first to believe that Jesus had truly risen from the dead.

---

1. http://legacyproject.org/guides/mdhistory.html, accessed 10/17/2011.

Atonement at Ground Zero

JOHN

> One of his disciples—the one whom Jesus loved—was reclining next to him. (John 13:23)

> Meanwhile, standing near the cross of Jesus were his mother, and his mother's sister, Mary the wife of Clopas, and Mary Magdalene. When Jesus saw his mother and the disciple whom he loved standing beside her, he said to his mother, "Woman, here is your son." Then he said to the disciple, "Here is your mother." And from that hour the disciple took her into his own home. (John 19:25–27)

> Early on the first day of the week, while it was still dark, Mary Magdalene came to the tomb and saw that the stone had been removed from the tomb. So she ran and went to Simon Peter and the other disciple, the one whom Jesus loved . . . (John 20:1–2)

> Peter turned and saw the disciple whom Jesus loved following them; he was the one who had reclined next to Jesus at the supper and had said, "Lord, who is it that is going to betray you?" When Peter saw him, he said to Jesus, "Lord, what about him?" Jesus said to him, "If it is my will that he remain until I come, what is that to you? Follow me!" So the rumor spread in the community that this disciple would not die. (John 21:20–23a)

∽

When the Beatles invaded the United States in 1964, it didn't take long for the adoring female fans to brand Paul McCartney as *the cute one*. You could love John, George, or Ringo, but only Paul would be identified with cuteness. McCartney is now seventy years old, still writing music and touring with his band, extending himself into multiple artistic endeavors, wealthy beyond his wildest dreams, and one of the most influential and prolific musicians in the world. Yet, in the hearts of millions of aging devotees, he remains *the cute one*.

Throughout church history, Jesus' friend John would remain *the beloved disciple*. There is ongoing scholarly debate about whether or not the references in John's Gospel to *the beloved disciple* are coded allusions to himself or to any of those within Jesus' close circle of friends.[2] Nevertheless, the moniker follows John more closely than it does any of the others.

---

2. In spite of historic tradition that equates John with the beloved disciple, contemporary scholars are not so sure: "In the second half of the gospel we meet the 'beloved

Friends, Family, and Followers

While John is viewed as one who enjoyed a particularly close relationship with Jesus, he shares with the other disciples a sense of confusion about Jesus' purpose and mission in the world. The Gospel accounts honestly describe the misunderstandings of Jesus' followers, and John is included in their ranks. John and his brother seemed to have a problem understanding the nature of power, and Jesus had to correct them more than once, as when they suggested a violent response to the rejection of Jesus by a village of Samaritans:

> When his disciples James and John saw it, they said, "Lord, do you want us to command fire to come down from heaven and consume them?" (Luke 9:54)

Jesus, of course, did not entertain their idea and got after them for coming up with it in the first place. Nevertheless, Jesus' affection and trust is ultimately made evident when he entrusts his own mother to "the disciple whom he loved." John's identification as that disciple may not be clear, but it was traditionally held in the early church that they were one and the same.[3]

The disciples of Jesus are sometimes portrayed in art as white-haired, elderly saints. They were, however, more likely to be Jesus' age or younger. Their bonding as friends and their love for Jesus would have the character that is unique to young men who share a common life and mission. The brutal death of Jesus and the scattering of the friends would have been devastating experiences for someone like John. The disillusionment and heartbreak would have run deep.

When I was sixteen years old, a young college student named Dana Millich began serving as an intern with the Campus Life[4] club that met on our campus. Dana was an athlete (a swimmer) and a musician (a guitar-

---

disciple..." Although numerous attempts have been made to equate the beloved disciple with John the son of Zebedee, on the basis of chapters 1–20 this is only a possible inference... Once again the beloved disciple *may* be linked with John the son of Zebedee, but this is not a necessary conclusion. It is in fact unlikely." Stanton, *The Gospels and Jesus*, 124.

3. The fourth-century historian Eusebius cites Polycrates, a second-century bishop: "John, who was both a witness and a teacher, who reclined upon the bosom of the Lord..." Eusebius, *Church History*, book V, chapter 24.2.

4. Ours was one of the first of these clubs in the late 1960's, and for a few years it enjoyed the status as the largest club on our public high school campus. For a Christian club, this was a unique time.

81

ist), and he made a point of taking an interest in the young people in our club. He came to my home a number of times and taught me new guitar techniques and, as a teenager trying to find my own sense of faith, the mentorship of this young leader meant a great deal to me.

The summer after his first year with our club, Dana was killed in a diving accident in New York while serving as a lifeguard at a camp. Hundreds of young people attended his funeral service and, as typical in a Christian gathering such as this, it was mixture of grief and joy. Dana would be deeply missed, but we rejoiced in his life and the hope that we would one day see him again.

I remember looking at Dana's body as it rested in the casket that day. As is often the case when viewing the embalmed and prepared bodies of those we have known and loved, it didn't really look like him, and I was shattered to see the lifeless form of this vibrant young man who had graciously shared his time and friendship with me only weeks earlier. It was the first time in my young life that I had lost someone who was not only close to me in age, but also close to me in friendship. I remember feeling lost that day, because a significant leader in my life was tragically taken from the world.

John's grief over the loss of Jesus would be magnified because of the violence and injustice that surrounded it. Jesus' death was not an accident; it was orchestrated and carried out with ruthless precision. Whether or not John was the only one referred to as *beloved*, it is clear from the Gospels that Jesus was beloved to John. It was, perhaps, that love that produced sufficient courage for John to approach the cross where Jesus was dying and to stand in support of Mary, who was losing her beloved son. John may have looked up at Jesus and recalled his words,

> "No one has greater love than this, to lay down one's life for one's friends." (John 15:13)

At that moment John might have heard something in his mind that would add to these words: *No one has greater love than this, to entrust one's mother to a beloved friend.* John would not be able to save his friend, but he could continue to serve him by caring for his mother.

At this point, the story would appear to be over for John just as it was for the others. Jesus was slipping away from them, and now they could only pick up the pieces of life that had been scattered like shards of broken pottery. John would have looked up at his dying friend and also seen the

Friends, Family, and Followers

two criminals dying on either side of him. Perhaps he would remember the misguided request that he and his brother James had made to Jesus, to reign with him on his right and left when he came into his kingdom—places now filled by men whose broken bodies would soon be crushed by Roman truncheons as the process of death was accelerated.

The deconstruction of John's concept of power and the evaporation of his hope in Jesus would create a fertility of the soul like the readiness that prepares a burnt-out forest to begin to rejuvenate its new life out of apparent barrenness. If John was indeed the beloved disciple to which his Gospel cryptically refers, then his arrival at the tomb after Mary's declaration that Jesus' body had been removed would have shaken his expectations even more than they had been up to the point of Jesus' death. It was one thing to put life back together, including bringing Mary into his home, and move through the grief and terror of the last few days. It was another to wait for what might be coming, to see what the authorities had up their conspiratorial sleeves with the removal of Jesus' body. It was not only a sacrilege to invade Jesus' tomb; it was also another tactic of fear.

Within a day John would encounter the risen Jesus. We are told that Mary Magdalene saw him first, but we don't know if the men in the group believed her. Once Jesus entered the room where they were gathered, they not only believed that he had been raised, but they also rejoiced that he was with them again.[5] The first words he speaks to them are not about what has happened to him, but rather about what will now happen to them.

> Again he said, "Peace be with you. As the Father has sent me, so I am sending you." Then he breathed on them and said, "Receive the Holy Spirit. If you forgive anyone's sins, they are forgiven. If you do not forgive them, they are not forgiven." (John 20:21–23, NLT)

If the disciples received any other information from Jesus about what his death has accomplished, John doesn't relay it in his account. Instead, Jesus' words to John and the others are about *sending*. Jesus identifies their commission with his own assignment given by his heavenly Father;

---

5. The only exception, of course, is Thomas, who was not in the room when Jesus appeared, and refused to believe his friends' story until he saw Jesus for himself. While Thomas has historically been labeled "Doubting Thomas," he does most of us a favor by speaking what we would have probably thought under the same circumstances. It should not miss our notice, however, that Thomas, once he sees Jesus for himself, offers one of the most profound declarations about Jesus to be found in the Bible: "My Lord and my God" (John 20:28).

he then empowers them by breathing the breath of God upon them, sending the Holy Spirit into their lives; he grants them the authority to forgive people their sins—an authority that could only come from God.

The focus for John appears to be on the power released in the lives of Jesus' followers after the resurrection. Jesus' death would have been a traumatic experience for John, yet in the Gospel attributed to him it is the new, empowered life that is highlighted. John's intention in relaying the story in the first place is not strictly to offer an historical account, but to engender faith and life in others:

> Now Jesus did many other signs in the presence of his disciples, which are not written in this book. But these are written so that you may come to believe that Jesus is the Messiah, the Son of God, and that through believing you may have life in his name. (John 20:30–31)

PETER

> "Simon, Simon, listen! Satan has demanded to sift all of you like wheat, but I have prayed for you that your own faith may not fail; and you, when once you have turned back, strengthen your brothers." And he said to him, "Lord, I am ready to go with you to prison and to death!" Jesus said, "I tell you, Peter, the cock will not crow this day, until you have denied three times that you know me." (Luke 22:31–34)

> The Lord turned and looked at Peter. Then Peter remembered the word of the Lord, how he had said to him, "Before the cock crows today, you will deny me three times." And he went out and wept bitterly. (Luke 22:61–62)

> He said to him the third time, "Simon son of John, do you love me?" Peter felt hurt because he said to him the third time, "Do you love me?" And he said to him, "Lord, you know everything; you know that I love you." Jesus said to him, "Feed my sheep. Very truly, I tell you, when you were younger, you used to fasten your own belt and to go wherever you wished. But when you grow old, you will stretch out your hands, and someone else will fasten a belt around you and take you where you do not wish to go." (He said this to indicate the kind of death by which he would glorify God.) After this he said to him, "Follow me." (John 21:17–19)

Friends, Family, and Followers

◈

No matter the overall integrity of one's life, one public failure has the power to permanently tattoo itself on a person's forehead. It isn't always the good things that history illuminates; the dramatic errors have the power to hit the headlines and stay imprinted on the popular mind.

Neville Chamberlain served in the British parliament for over twenty years, three of those as Prime Minister. While he had his political opponents, he was generally respected as an able and trustworthy politician. There was much to be respected about Neville Chamberlain.

The focus of history, however, is on Chamberlain's acquiescence to the demands of Adolf Hitler and his weak response to Germany's aggressive actions that led to World War II. The rest of Chamberlain's life fades into the mist as his failure as Britain's Prime Minister from 1937–1940 takes center stage. His successor, Winston Churchill, paid tribute to Chamberlain after his death in 1940, but even Churchill's generous words reflect on the weak responses that opened the way for Hitler to decimate Europe:

> . . . It fell to Neville Chamberlain in one of the supreme crises of the world to be contradicted by events, to be disappointed in his hopes, and to be deceived and cheated by a wicked man. But what were these hopes in which he was disappointed? What were these wishes in which he was frustrated? What was that faith that was abused? They were surely among the most noble and benevolent instincts of the human heart—the love of peace, the toil for peace, the strife for peace, the pursuit of peace, even at great peril and certainly in utter disdain of popularity or clamor.[6]

Chamberlain, for the most part, lived a good life. What we remember the most, however, are his failed negotiations with one of the worst tyrants the world has ever seen.

The New Testament tells us a great deal about Peter. He was one of the first disciples to be called by Jesus and was in his inner circle of friends; he was brash but deeply loyal to Jesus; he preached the first post-Pentecost sermon and served the emerging church as a leader until his death; he was the first to experience God's favor on the Gentiles and convinced the church leaders in Jerusalem that God was doing new and wonderful things. Peter is also characterized as brash and impetuous,

---

6. Shirer, *The Rise and Fall of the Third Reich*, 619.

expressing misguided demonstrations of loyalty and violence.[7] Even after Jesus' resurrection and ascension, Peter brings his own brand of leadership to bear on the community of believers. He decides that the place among the twelve disciples that was vacated by Judas must be filled, and the community agrees:

> Then they prayed and said, "Lord, you know everyone's heart. Show us which one of these two you have chosen to take the place in this ministry and apostleship from which Judas turned aside to go to his own place." And they cast lots for them, and the lot fell on Matthias; and he was added to the eleven apostles. (Acts 1:24–26)

The significance of this decision is unclear to us, because immediately after being chosen, Matthias disappears from the story and is never heard from again. It could indeed have been just one of those unexplained mysteries of God; it could also be Peter's desire to do something that would get things moving again. Perhaps he concluded that God was waiting to act until the twelfth empty seat at the table was filled again. It would not be out of character for Peter to suggest such action.

We don't really forget those aspects of Peter's story, but the event we remember the most is Peter's three denials of Jesus. It wasn't at the hands of Roman interrogators that Peter disavowed any knowledge of Jesus; it was the result of the questioning by some servants:

> Then they seized [Jesus] and led him away, bringing him into the high priest's house. But Peter was following at a distance. When they had kindled a fire in the middle of the courtyard and sat down together, Peter sat among them. Then a servant-girl, seeing him in the firelight, stared at him and said, "This man also was with him." But he denied it, saying, "Woman, I do not know him." A little later someone else, on seeing him, said, "You also are one of them." But Peter said, "Man, I am not!" Then about an hour later yet another kept insisting, "Surely this man also was with him; for he is a Galilean." But Peter said, "Man, I do not know what you are talking about!" At that moment, while he was still speaking, the cock crowed. (Luke 22:54–60)

All four Gospels chronicle Peter's failure—no one leaves his story out. In the Synoptics, Peter appears after his denials only briefly to inspect

---

7. As in his attack on the high priest's slave in John 18:10–11.

the empty tomb. It's almost as if the Gospel writers thought it fitting to end Peter's story at that point.

There is no mention in the New Testament of Peter hovering anywhere near the execution site where Jesus died. We don't know where Peter was hiding, but it's likely he wished that an avalanche would pour down the side of a mountain and hide him forever. Peter was the one always barking courageously about his commitment to Jesus, even to death. Peter sought to protect his dear friend from harm, yet at his darkest moment, he deserted Jesus out of fear.

Peter would not have seen forgiveness for the sins of the world radiating from that cross. The image of Jesus dying would not translate for Peter into a theological paradigm of sacrifice, substitution, or victory. Instead, he would have seen his greatest failure in life because he couldn't protect his friend and even lost courage at the end. It is no wonder that Peter was not to be found at the scene of the crucifixion. How could he stand near Jesus' mother and look up at the one he had deserted who was now dying horribly? How could he walk shoulder-to-shoulder with the other disciple—the one called *beloved*—who had not cowered in fear? Peter propelled himself from the fellowship of Jesus because of the power of shame—it told him he was excluded from the place where he longed to be.

∽

According to biblical scholars, the authorship of the New Testament letters of First and Second Peter is uncertain.[8] Some say that Peter himself dictated the letters to a well-educated scribe (since Peter is characterized along with John in Acts 4:13 as "uneducated and ordinary"); others suggest that the letters were written posthumously based on the familiar teachings of the apostle. While we cannot know with certainty whether or not Peter directly wrote the letters, it does appear that the early church accepted the letters on the basis of Peter's authority as an apostle.

---

8. J. Ramsey Michaels echoes this view regarding First Peter, since it appears that Second Peter is considered by many to be the product of a later Christian community. "As in the case of most NT books other than the letters of Paul, the discussion of the authorship of 1 Peter is a futile discussion if its purpose is anything approaching absolute certainty." Michaels, *1 Peter*, lxii.

If, at the very least, these two letters are imbedded with Peter's influence, then they express his own theological reflection on the significance of the death of Jesus:

> Blessed be the God and Father of our Lord Jesus Christ! By his great mercy he has given us a new birth into a living hope through the resurrection of Jesus Christ from the dead, and into an inheritance that is imperishable, undefiled, and unfading, kept in heaven for you, who are being protected by the power of God through faith for a salvation ready to be revealed in the last time. (I Peter 1:3–5)

> He himself bore our sins in his body on the cross, so that, free from sins, we might live for righteousness; by his wounds you have been healed. (I Peter 2:24)

> For Christ also suffered for sins once for all, the righteous for the unrighteous, in order to bring you to God. He was put to death in the flesh, but made alive in the spirit . . . (II Peter 3:18)

The views ascribed to the apostle Peter—the same Peter who turned his face from the dying Jesus out of fear and shame—now ring with claims about a living hope, a salvation ready to be revealed, freedom to live for righteousness, and the gift of being brought to God. It appears that for Peter and the community that treasured his authority, the death of Jesus did not stand alone; it was eternally linked to resurrection, and resulted in a new kind of life for his followers.

For one whose story of cowardice was well known, Peter would clearly have luxuriated in the realization that the death of Jesus was not the end of the drama. Freedom from sins, for Peter, would surely have included his denial of the one who had always loved him.

JUDAS

> And [Jesus] appointed twelve, whom he also named apostles, to be with him, and to be sent out to proclaim the message, and to have authority to cast out demons. So he appointed the twelve . . . and Judas Iscariot, who betrayed him. (Mark 3:14–16a, 19)

> Then one of the twelve, who was called Judas Iscariot, went to the chief priests and said, "What will you give me if I betray him to

Friends, Family, and Followers

you?" They paid him thirty pieces of silver. And from that moment he began to look for an opportunity to betray him.

(Matt 26:14–16)

Then Satan entered into Judas called Iscariot . . . (Luke 22:3a)

So when [Jesus] had dipped the piece of bread, he gave it to Judas son of Simon Iscariot. (John 13:26b)

When Judas, his betrayer, saw that Jesus was condemned, he repented and brought back the thirty pieces of silver to the chief priests and the elders. He said, "I have sinned by betraying innocent blood." But they said, "What is that to us? See to it yourself." Throwing down the pieces of silver in the temple, he departed; and he went and hanged himself. (Matt 27:3–5)

I recently planted two trees in my yard. Their botanical name is *Cercis Canadensis*, commonly known as Eastern Redbud. One of the unique features of these lovely, pink-flowered trees is the frailty of their branches—their weak woodedness. Legend has it that Judas Iscariot hanged himself from such a tree as these, and since that day so long ago the species refuses to grow branches strong enough to bear the weight of another who might wish to commit suicide by hanging. That is why it is known as *the Judas tree*.

Look up the name *Judas* in any dictionary and you'll see at least two definitions: One naming the disciple, the other as a label for a betrayer. One of the other disciples, also named Judas, receives a generous clarification of his identity in John's Gospel, where he is called "Judas (not Iscariot)" (John 13:22a). John was quick to make sure there was no confusion on that point. One would never want to be identified as the wrong Judas.

There is a lot that we do not know about Judas. Even the moniker *Iscariot* offers little help. Scholars suggest all kinds of possibilities for the label, none of which are conclusive.[9] Over two thousand years, however, the name *Judas* suffices and it conjures up images of the ultimate in traitors, evil incarnate, a thief, a godless opportunist, and any number of other descriptors of evil. A characterization that is not specifically identified in

---

9. Suggestions regarding the meaning of the modifier Iscariot include "a man of Kerioth," "Man of Issachar," and "the assassin." Williams, "Judas Iscariot," 406.

the New Testament but is made clear at the first calling of the disciples is one that must also be considered when talking about Judas.

He was an answer to Jesus' prayer.

In Matthew chapter four, Jesus isolates himself for forty days in the wilderness. While the account of his time there is dominated by his wrestling with the temptations to wield power by popular demand, one can assume that a prolonged period of fasting and prayer in the absence of human interaction would be intense. Matthew offers some words of comfort at the end of the story:

> Then the devil left him, and suddenly angels came and waited on him. (Matt 4:11)

What would Jesus wrestle with in prayer? Certainly he struggled with his own sense of destiny and how that would be walked out; that struggle is made clear in the relaying of the three temptations. It seems doubtful that Jesus would return to the world of people and randomly select twelve men to follow him by flipping a coin or picking the first ones he encountered, getting things horribly wrong in choosing Judas. The text suggests otherwise, because immediately following the wilderness account, Matthew describes Jesus taking two significant actions: He begins declaring his core message of the presence of the kingdom of heaven (4:17), and he calls his disciples (4:18–22), including Judas. Luke is even more succinct:

> Now during those days he went out to the mountain to pray; and he spent the night in prayer to God. And when day came, he called his disciples and chose twelve of them, whom he also named apostles: Simon, whom he named Peter, and his brother Andrew, and James, and John, and Philip, and Bartholomew, and Matthew, and Thomas, and James son of Alphaeus, and Simon, who was called the Zealot, and Judas son of James, and Judas Iscariot, who became a traitor. (Luke 6:12–16)

Imperfect, broken, and driven by self-interest, Judas joined this band of brothers at the bidding of Jesus, who called the twelve to be his closest friends and followers. And he did this as a response to a night of prayer.[10]

---

10. "What is clear and unavoidable in this account of the choosing of the twelve is that Jesus prayed all night and then chose the twelve in full assurance that these twelve had been *given* him by the Father in answer to prayer. However difficult and unreliable the twelve might become, Jesus would always consider them given to Him by the Father."

Like the others, Judas would have had conflicted intentions when it came to Jesus. He shared with others the misperception that Jesus would be a leader who would restore Israel to greatness and would do so by overthrowing the Romans. James and John tried to posture themselves for power; Peter was ready to fight anyone who threatened Jesus; Matthew left a successful if not corrupt tax practice and might have wondered if he was betting on the wrong horse.

Judas, of course, actually conspired with the Jewish authorities to help them take Jesus into custody at a time when the crowds would not be gathered around him so that they could act in secret. On top of that, Judas took money in exchange for the information. It appears that Judas simply did not care whether or not Jesus was left to the devices of his enemies.

Or did he?

In Matthew chapter twenty-seven, realizing that his act of betrayal has turned into the condemnation of Jesus, Judas tries to undo what he has done. He tells the Jewish leaders that he has "sinned by betraying innocent blood." What in the world was Judas trying to accomplish in the first place? Perhaps he thought that Jesus was too slow in bringing his revolutionary agenda to bear upon Israel, and was betting that the community leaders might be able to accelerate the process. Or maybe Judas was tired of following Jesus around and waiting for something to happen that matched his personal agenda. One thing is clear from Matthew's account: Judas never intended for Jesus to be condemned to death.

Judas was not entirely alone in his duplicity. At Jesus' arrest, most of the disciples disappeared from the scene. Peter turned his back in fear. Even the crowds, who had earlier welcomed Jesus into the city as he rode on a donkey, now screamed for his death. We probably paint Judas with the darkest brush because of his intentionality in conspiring with Jesus' enemies. That's what traitors do.

Once Judas realized his mistake, it was too late for both he and Jesus. Judas did not allow himself to return to his former friends and ask forgiveness. He must have assumed that his act of betrayal would forever ban him from their fellowship. He couldn't throw himself at Jesus' feet because those feet were about to be nailed to a cross. In the death that he had helped to facilitate, Judas leaves the story with his final descriptive words: *Innocent blood.*

Anderson, *The Gospel According to Judas: Is There a Limit to God's Forgiveness?*, 47.

If there was ever any perception about Jesus' death being a get-out-of-jail card for sin, then Judas missed it. He did not see what he had done as part of the overarching plan of God, a plan in which Judas played a key part. Instead, he saw it as a major collapse, and now one who was innocent was about to be unjustly executed. What was Judas to do?

The only thing left for him to do was to appeal to the Jewish leaders. These were men well schooled in Jewish worship practices and liturgy. They knew how forgiveness worked and how to lead the people of Israel into practices of atonement for sin. Judas returned the money, hoping to reverse the process of death, but received indifference from the leaders. The only counsel they gave to him was heard by Judas as an invitation to suicide:

"What is that to us? See to it yourself."

How does one like Judas do that? How does he see to his own absolution? He was excluded from all possible places of hope: Proximity to Jesus, the fellowship of the disciples, and the care of the Jewish leadership. In his mind, his despair would leave him with only one option, and his death would precede that of the one he had betrayed.

How could one follow Jesus for three years, sharing in his ministry (even proclaiming the good news of the kingdom and casting out demons!), receiving the elements of the Last Supper, and then make what he perceives as a tragic, unforgiveable error? What was it about Judas' perception of Jesus and his impending death that made it impossible for him to see that death as an event that would guarantee forgiveness? What was it that Paul understood that Judas never seemed to grasp?

> So if anyone is in Christ, there is a new creation: everything old has passed away; see, everything has become new! All this is from God, who reconciled us to himself through Christ, and has given us the ministry of reconciliation; that is, in Christ God was reconciling the world to himself, not counting their trespasses against them . . . (2 Cor 5:17–19a)

One thing is clear: For Judas, the death of Jesus was the end of it all.

Friends, Family, and Followers

THE EMMAUS TRAVELERS

> Now on that same day two of them were going to a village called Emmaus, about seven miles from Jerusalem, and talking with each other about all these things that had happened. While they were talking and discussing, Jesus himself came near and went with them, but their eyes were kept from recognizing him. (Luke 24:13–16)

> Then he said to them. "Oh, how foolish you are, and how slow of heart to believe all that the prophets have declared! Was it not necessary that the Messiah should suffer these things and then enter into his glory?" Then beginning with Moses and all the prophets, he interpreted to them the things about himself in all the Scriptures. (Luke 24:25–27)

> They said to each other, "Were not our hearts burning within us…?" (Luke 24:32a)

Numerous artists have depicted the Emmaus scene in paintings. Two very striking versions were created by the 17th-century Italian artist Michelangelo Merisi da Caravaggio. The first painting, titled "Supper at Emmaus," depicts Jesus at the table with his two companions, with a servant or innkeeper looking on. The picture is one of sharp, detailed clarity, from the facial expressions of the people to the claws on the feet of the roasted game bird on the table. The moment that has been frozen in time is the point at which the men recognize that it is Jesus who has been walking and dining with them. The innkeeper looks on with an expression of intense curiosity, while the two at the table appear to be about to leap up and start a brawl. It is a scene of shocking vividness as the fog clears from their eyes and they finally see the face of Jesus before them.

About four years later, Caravaggio produced a second painting with the same title. This time, however, the light and details of the scene at the table soften, as do the reactions of the people to the revelation of Jesus' presence among them. The innkeeper is now joined by a woman at his side, and both show mild interest in the exchange among the men. The two at the table seemed surprised, but not shocked with the melodramatic effect of the first painting. Jesus looks very different in this depiction. Rather than the clean-shaven, cherubic face of the first version, he looks more human, more approachable, more earthy than in the original. In the first, he appears feminine, plump, and detached from the others at the table. In the second, he looks like a young Eric Clapton engaged in deep conversation with his rugged friends. This Jesus looks like he's been walking on a dusty road and could use a good meal.

The episode on the road to Emmaus appears only in Luke's Gospel. It reads in a way that makes Caravaggio's second painting more believable than the first. It is a very solemn, human story of people left devastated by the recent events surrounding Jesus' death and, in the midst of their grief and disillusionment, trying to make sense of it all. As the unrecognized Jesus joins them, they describe to him what had happened when he asks what they are discussing among themselves.

> "The things about Jesus of Nazareth, who was a prophet mighty in deed and word before God and all the people, and how our chief priests and leaders handed him over to be condemned to death and crucified him." (Luke 24:19b-20)

Their account is straightforward, direct, and without interpretation. Cleopas is a new figure in the Gospel story,[11] and he and his unnamed companion disappear after the account wraps up. They were likely part of the larger groups of disciples that were not considered part of the original twelve, and had followed closely the events of Jesus' arrest and crucifixion. They report to Jesus that the women of their company discovered the empty tomb and were encountered by angels, and then "Some of those who were with us went to the tomb and found it just as the women had said; but they did not see him" (Luke 24:24).

In their state of disorientation—after witnessing Jesus' arrest, condemnation, crucifixion, death, and now reports of the empty tomb—the two grieving disciples confess their belief that Jesus was not the one they had hoped he would be:

> "But we had hoped that he was the one to redeem Israel." (Luke 24:21)

The one part of the story that seems odd is the apparent inability of the men to recognize Jesus. Were they sufficiently distant from the inner circle of Jesus that they had never spent time with him in intimate conversation so that his face would be emblazoned on their minds? Or were they so immersed in grief that they couldn't find the energy to make

---

11. Perhaps the same "Clopas" of John 19:25.

eye contact with the wandering stranger who had joined them on the road? Or, did God simply cloud their eyes so they couldn't see Jesus and recognize him?

When my wife and I were first married, we made friends with a young couple who had also just married. As often happens, we both pursued different life demands in our work, and lost touch for about a year. One day, Emily and I were walking through the parking lot of a local mall when a man came up to us and greeted us by name. Neither of us recognized him as our friend from a year earlier, because this man looked thin, gaunt, and years older than the one we remembered. It turned out that his young wife had left him and he almost withdrew to his bed and let himself die. It was only the intervention of the people at his church that helped him find some new place of life after the traumatic events of the last year. We failed to recognize our friend because our expectations were embedded in an old reality.

I wonder if, like Mary who thought Jesus was the gardener near the tomb (John 20:15), the two men on the Emmaus road had no framework of expectation that would allow them to recognize the one who had just been brutally beaten and nailed to a cross. If there was any image burned into their brains, it would have been of a bloodied, broken corpse rather than of a jaunty traveler eager for conversation. Regardless of the reason for their lack of recognition, the scene becomes the occasion for Jesus to school these faithful men in how the events of his death and resurrection were the apex of the entire scriptural narrative.

It seems significant that Jesus did not suddenly become known to the men because of the realization that this death had a theological interpretation or a salvific effect. He became known to them as he broke the bread on the table before them, an act that was not only familiar but also the preparation for sharing the gift of physical nourishment together. Their eyes no longer saw the crucified, destroyed, would-be Messiah; they now saw the risen Jesus, who sat with them at the table, preparing to enact one of the most fundamental rituals of life. Upon his disappearance from their midst, they acted as though hope had returned to them:

> That same hour they got up and returned to Jerusalem; and they found the eleven and their companions gathered together. They were saying, "The Lord has risen indeed, and he has appeared to Simon!" Then they told what had happened on the road, and how he had been made known to them in the breaking of the bread. (Luke 24:33–35)

PAUL

> Then they dragged [Stephen] out of the city and began to stone him; and the witnesses laid their coats at the feet of a young man named Saul. (Acts 7:58)

> Now as [Saul] was going along and approaching Damascus, suddenly a light from heaven flashed around him. He fell to the ground and heard a voice saying to him, "Saul, Saul, why do you persecute me?" He asked, "Who are you, Lord?" The reply came, "I am Jesus, whom you are persecuting. But get up and enter the city, and you will be told what you are to do." (Acts 9:3–6)

> For the love of Christ urges us on, because we are convinced that one has died for all; therefore all have died. And he died for all, so that those who live might live no longer for themselves, but for him who died and was raised for them. (2 Cor 5:14–16)

～

There are any number of reasons why a person might want a change of name. I knew of a financial consultant who advised his young physician client to legally change his name before opening his new medical practice in southern California. The young man was born and raised in India, and his name was perfectly acceptable in that context. In the United States, however, the name would be heard as comically profane. The young doctor took the advice and it served him well.

Norma Jeane Baker, Vincent Furnier, Gordon Sumner, and Paul Hewson became Marilyn Monroe, Alice Cooper, Sting, and Bono as part of their celebrity personas. People might change their names in order to distance themselves from family scandals or because of breaks in relationship. Names are only words, but they become inseparable from the identities and characters of the people they label.

We don't know why Paul changed his name from his given name, Saul. We are only told that he was "... Saul, also known as Paul ..." (Acts 13:9). The name Saul would have identified him with his hometown (as in Saul of Tarsus), and also with the famous ancient king of Israel. At some point, however, he began to use the new name. While his choice might have been based on a variety of motivations—the need to hide from his enemies or to assuage the suspicions of the Christians he formerly persecuted; to create an identity with the Gentiles he hoped to reach; or as a sign of his new life in Christ—the name change has always symbolized the dramatic shift in Paul's life.

As far as we know, Paul did not see Jesus die. If he did, the New Testament makes no mention of it. Maybe Paul did not stand at ground zero, but he was at least one ripple away from the point of impact. We first meet Paul (as the young man Saul) as he guards the coats of those who stoned Stephen to death.[12] Paul also did not encounter Jesus as the resurrected Lord. He did not view the empty tomb and then experience the subsequent appearances of Jesus that were reported by the disciples of Jesus. It was after the resurrection appearances had ceased that Jesus—the ascended Lord and Christ—overwhelmed the young Pharisee on the road to Damascus, conscripting him into God's mission in the world. Paul himself describes the chronology of events:

> For I handed on to you as of first importance what I in turn had received: that Christ died for our sins in accordance with the Scriptures, and that he was buried, and that he was raised on the third day in accordance with the Scriptures, and that he appeared to Cephas, then to the twelve. Then he appeared to more than five hundred brothers and sisters at one time, most of whom are still alive, though some have died. Then he appeared to James, then to all the apostles. Last of all, as to someone untimely born, he appeared also to me. For I am the least of the apostles, unfit to be called an apostle, because I persecuted the church of God. (1 Cor 15:3–9)

Paul was a young, rising star in the Jewish community. His zeal for Israel and her destiny as God's people would certainly have fueled his anger toward the apparently errant Jews who had followed a failed Messiah and were risking the integrity of the faith. Was a freakishly blinding experience on the open road enough to convert him to the cause he had so vehemently opposed? What might have been going on in his head that resulted in the radical change that altered the trajectory of his life?

N. T. Wright offers this scholarly insight into Saul/Paul's conversion experience:

> The significance of Jesus' resurrection, for Saul of Tarsus as he lay blinded and perhaps bruised on the road to Damascus, was this. *The one true God had done for Jesus of Nazareth, in the middle of time, what Saul had thought he was going to do for Israel at the*

---

12. His approval of Stephen's death suggests that he would have also approved of the death of Jesus.

> *end of time.* Saul had imagined that YHWH would vindicate *Israel* after her suffering at the hand of the pagans. Instead, he had vindicated *Jesus* after his suffering at the hand of the pagans. Saul had imagined that the great reversal, the great apocalyptic event, would take place all at once, inaugurating the kingdom of God with a flourish of trumpets, setting all wrongs to right, defeating evil once and for all, and ushering in the age to come. Instead, the great reversal, the great resurrection, had happened to one man, all by himself.[13]

The story of Saul's conversion in Acts chapter nine requires us to consider the possibility that there was much more going on than a change in his way of thinking. This was not simply a reconstruction of a religious paradigm, but an engagement with the Spirit of God that was beyond Saul's immediate comprehension. When the Damascene disciple Ananias is commissioned by God to care for Saul, he reluctantly obeys and does what may have become normative for those being welcomed into the company of Jesus.

> He laid his hands on Saul and said, "Brother Saul, the Lord Jesus, who appeared to you on your way here, has sent me so that you may regain your sight and be filled with the Holy Spirit." And immediately something like scales fell from his eyes, and his sight was restored. Then he got up and was baptized, and after taking some food, he regained his strength. (Acts 9:17b-19a)

You can hear this experience echoed through Paul's later words to the church in Rome:

> I appeal to you therefore, brothers and sisters, by the mercies of God, to present your bodies as a living sacrifice, holy and acceptable to God, which is your spiritual worship. Do not be conformed to this world, but be transformed by the renewing of your minds, so that you may discern what is the will of God—what is good and acceptable and perfect. (Rom 12:1-2)

For someone who did not see the death of Jesus take place, Paul certainly does speak of death and the cross a great deal in his writings. He was distanced from the ground zero of Jesus' crucifixion, which may be why he was the first to develop and communicate significant theological interpretations of that death. The cross of Jesus made a significant impact on Paul, yet he describes the effect of that death in a variety of ways:

13. Wright, *What Saint Paul Really Said*, 36.

- Jesus died on behalf of all broken human beings, none of whom could do for themselves what only God could do. (Rom 5:6–11)
- The cross is foolishness to all except those who are brought together by faith in Christ. (1 Cor 1:18–25)
- It foreshadows how Jesus' followers will die to the religious forces of the world that seek to define righteousness by something humans can do for themselves. (Gal 6:12–16)
- It represents the Gospel for Paul. (Phil 3:17–18)
- The cross results in the reconciliation of all things. (Col 1:15–20)
- It symbolizes the disempowering of religious legalism as well as the disarming of the dominant powers of the world. (Col 2:8–15)

Paul, as an outsider to the events of the cross, may have found it necessary to emphasize the crucifixion to make sure his audiences understood that he was speaking of the real, historic Jesus—the one crucified on a particular Roman cross at a particular point in time—and not merely offering speculation based in mysticism or mere theological acrobatics. From his vantage point outside of ground zero, Paul was a Jewish scholar and, as such, he would have to dive deeply into what was going on with the death of Jesus and his subsequent resurrection. He would not abandon his understanding of Israel's destiny and the expectation of God's vindication, but would instead reframe his thinking around Jesus in terms of God's victory over sin, evil, and death. Once again, N. T. Wright helps us with this:

> . . . I suggest that we give priority—a priority among equals, perhaps, but still a priority—to those Pauline expressions of the crucifixion of Jesus which describe it as the decisive victory over the "principalities and powers". Nothing in the many other expressions of the meaning of the cross is lost if we put this in the centre. . . . The death of Jesus had the effect of liberating both Jew and Gentile from the enslaving force of the "elements of the world" (Gal 4:1–11). And, towering over almost everything else, the death of Jesus, seen as the culmination of his great act of obedience, is the means whereby the reign of sin and death is replaced with the reign of grace and righteousness (Rom 5:12–21). "The gospel" is indeed the announcement of royal victory.[14]

14. Ibid., 47.

Atonement at Ground Zero

When Paul chronicles his own history of persecuting the church (which, in Acts 9, Jesus equates with persecuting *him*) his confessions suggest a deep sense of guilt mixed with the joy of the new life he has found in Christ. No, he did not stand at the foot of the cross and mock the suffering and death of Jesus, but he may as well have done so. As one "untimely born," however, he came to the faith not only late, in relation to the earlier disciples, but also prematurely, experiencing Jesus as the ascended Lord, just as millions of others would do over the next 2,000 years.[15]

---

15. The reference in 1 Cor 15:8 about Paul's "untimely" birth may actually be one that means early (premature) rather than late. As N. T. Wright comments, "This is a violent image, invoking the idea of a Caesarian section, in which a baby is ripped from the womb, born before it is ready, blinking in shock at the sudden light, scarcely able to breathe in this new world." Wright, *The Challenge of Easter*, 21.

9

Jesus of Nazareth

> While they were eating, Jesus took a loaf of bread, and after blessing it he broke it, gave it to the disciples, and said, "Take, eat; this is my body." Then he took a cup, and after giving thanks he gave it to them, saying, "Drink from it, all of you; for this is my blood of the covenant, which is poured out for many for the forgiveness of sins." (Matt 26:26–28)
>
> At three o'clock Jesus cried out with a loud voice, "Eloi, Eloi, lema sabachthani?" which means, "My God, my God, why have you forsaken me?" (Mark 15:34)
>
> Then Jesus said, "Father, forgive them; for they do not know what they are doing." (Luke 23:34)

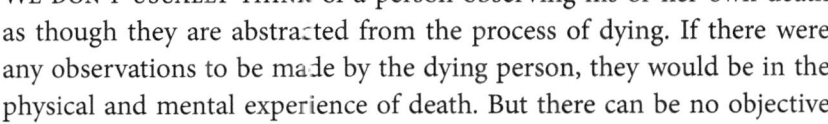

WE DON'T USUALLY THINK of a person observing his or her own death as though they are abstracted from the process of dying. If there were any observations to be made by the dying person, they would be in the physical and mental experience of death. But there can be no objective analysis about death when you are the one dying. The person whose life is draining away is fully immersed in the process.

Indeed, Jesus was present at his own death. He not only anticipated his death but was also denied the distance of external observation. People who are conscious as they die might express a variety of responses to impending death, ranging from accepting the inevitabilities of old age or illness, to outrage that such an injustice was taking place. Jesus, however, had very different responses.

Certainly Jesus understood the danger he was courting as he confronted the religious authorities of Israel. Even his followers were aware of the precarious situation they were in as friends of Jesus. In one of Jesus' predictions of his death, the Gospel of Mark claims that he spoke to the disciples because they were afraid (Mark 10:32). As Thomas remarked when Jesus set out for Bethany to raise Lazarus from the grave,

> "Let us also go, that we may die with him." (John 11:16)

While Matthew, Mark, and Luke offer their versions of the scene where Jesus predicts his death, each includes a reference to his anticipated resurrection (Matt 20:17–19, Mark 10:32–34, Luke 18:31–34). In Matthew 26, however, the link between death and resurrection is made more cryptically than in the others. Jesus very clearly predicts what is about to happen to him:

> When Jesus had finished saying all these things, he said to his disciples, "You know that after two days the Passover is coming, and the Son of Man will be handed over to be crucified." (Matt 26:1–2)

While the reference to his impending death is clear and startling, his interpretation of that death comes in the sharing of the Passover meal with his disciples:

> While they were eating, Jesus took a loaf of bread, and after blessing it he broke it, gave it to the disciples, and said, "Take, eat; this is my body." Then he took a cup, and after giving thanks he gave it to them, saying, "Drink from it, all of you; for this is my blood of the covenant, which is poured out for many for the forgiveness of sins. I tell you, I will never again drink of this fruit of the vine until that day when I drink it new with you in my Father's kingdom." (Matt 26:26–29)

Jesus might have expected that retributive action on the part of both Israel and Rome would result in his death, and crucifixion was the sure way of execution. Caiaphas offered his perspective on Jesus' death ("... it is better for you to have one man die for the people than to have the whole nation destroyed"), revealing his conviction that Jesus would serve as a representative of the seditious side of Israel, giving Rome a substitute to punish rather than the entire nation. Jesus' understanding is very different from that. He uses the language of covenant, and describes his representative death in terms of forgiveness of sins. His words carry echoes of Jeremiah 31:

> The days are surely coming, says the Lord, when I will make a new covenant with the house of Israel and the house of Judah. It will not be like the covenant that I made with their ancestors when I took them by the hand to bring them out of the land of Egypt—a covenant that they broke, though I was their husband, says the Lord. But this is the covenant that I will make with the house of Israel after those days, says the Lord: I will put my law within them, and I will write it on their hearts; and I will be their God, and they shall be my people. No longer shall they teach one another, or say to each other, "Know the Lord", for they shall all know me, from the least of them to the greatest, says the Lord; for I will forgive their iniquity, and remember their sin no more. (Jer 31:31–34)

Clearly, Jesus saw his death as something more than another injustice perpetrated against the prophets of Israel. He understood his identity as Israel's true Messiah,[1] and as such he would represent the people of God. This representation, however, would not be in terms of leading a power play that would unseat the Romans and liberate Israel to her rightful place in the world, but rather in the revealing of God's new covenant, one that forgave the people their sins.

It is significant that Jesus spoke these words at a Passover meal, the table shared by Jews everywhere. In the words of covenant and forgiveness, faithful Jews anticipated the great banquet feast that would mark God's new work in Israel.[2] In the original Passover, God brought Israel's liberation from bondage, empowering Moses to bring leadership. At this new table, however, God's new work of liberation comes in and through Jesus, and it comes as Jesus submits his body to the worst that the world

---

1. As evidenced by his conversation with the woman of Samaria: "The woman said to him, 'I know that Messiah is coming' (who is called Christ). 'When he comes, he will proclaim all things to us.' Jesus said to her, 'I am he, the one who is speaking to you'" (John 4:25–26).

2. In reference to the Last Supper, N. T. Wright affirms this forward look: "This is regularly, and rightly, seen as a symbolic evocation of the coming messianic banquet, perhaps already anticipated by the community that awaits the final consummation." Wright, *Jesus and the Victory of God*, 532.

can do. At the table with his disciples, Jesus represents God to Israel and fully identifies with his disciples.[3]

As he dies, however, he also represents the people to God. In one of his final utterances on the cross, one that we explored earlier from the perspective of the Centurion at the cross, Jesus cries out his deep identification with Israel:

> "My God, my God, why have you forsaken me?"

Some have speculated that in his lonely cry, Jesus is experiencing the complete and utter abandonment of God as the Heavenly Father turns his face from the Son. However, this cry of Jesus is not one conjured up spontaneously in the agony of death. As we saw earlier, his words are a direct quote from a text that would be familiar to the Jews who were within hearing.

> My God, my God, why have you forsaken me? Why are you so far from helping me, from the words of my groaning? O my God, I cry by day, but you do not answer; and by night, but find no rest. (Ps 22:1–2)

Jesus cries out the words of an Israel in exile, one that wonders when deliverance will ever come. In that cry he fully identifies himself with his fellow Jews, and cries before God the cry that has resonated through the people of Israel for centuries—the cry for God's deliverance and forgiveness of his people.

The representational role of Jesus is staggering in its breadth. Through the eyes of God's anointed One, he looks down in agony at the people he has come to save. He acts as the agent of God, demonstrating God's love and mission in all that he is, even to his dying breath. He hangs on the cross in three other roles as well. On the cross he represents the righteous of Israel as the perfect Israelite in whom there is no sin. He is there in innocence, falsely accused, judged, and condemned, all the while maintaining his faithfulness to God. Jesus also represents the unrighteous of Israel as he hangs between two criminals, sharing death in solidarity with them, and embracing the one who will accompany him into paradise.

---

3. "Drinking the cup is a gesture analogous to daubing one's house with blood. It identifies the disciples with Jesus. Because the bread and the wine stand for his body and blood, partaking of them is the means of a new kind of oneness with Jesus. It makes Jesus part of our life in the most concrete way and makes us part of Jesus' life (Jn 6:52–57)." Goldingay, *Old Testament Theology*, 835.

Jesus of Nazareth

There is a third role that Jesus plays as he dies. Just as Israel itself represented the entire world to God, and through them blessing would flow to all the families of the earth (Gen 12:1–2), so does Jesus represent the world before God. This global representation would quickly find expression in the life of the early church, as they would come to understand the universal nature of what God had done in Jesus:

> ... he is the atoning sacrifice for our sins, and not for ours only but also for the sins of the whole world. (1 John 2:2)

Certainly the first Christians would hear the stories of the Holy Spirit falling upon the God-fearing Gentiles in Antioch (Acts 10–11) and work through the letters of Paul that would circulate among the churches. They would come to understand that the story God was writing was larger and more expansive than they had ever imagined. But that part of the story didn't emerge from an isolated incident in Antioch, nor did the apostle Paul craft it out of his own theological imagination. It came from the voice of Jesus as he plummeted toward death, nailed to the cross by Jew and Gentile alike:

> "Father, forgive them; for they do not know what they are doing."

Soon Jesus would die. In that death he made it clear that somehow, he died for all.

PART THREE

Metaphors and Meaning

10

Moving from the Past toward the Future

> For now we see through a glass, darkly; but then face to face: now I know in part; but then shall I know even as also I am known. (1 Cor 13:12, KJV)

ASPECTS OF THE PRIMARY models of the atonement that have dominated Christian thinking over the centuries—Recapitulation, Christus Victor, Satisfaction, and Substitution—are found in our Scriptures and find interpretation in particular cultural frameworks. How does looking at ground zero help us consider new images for the atonement that speak today in concert with the narrative of Scripture?

What do the narratives of the New Testament provide in terms of perceptions of the death of Jesus? The various witnesses to the event of Jesus' crucifixion offer us some important points of view.

Caiaphas and Pilate would agree that it served the larger good that one man was substituted so that others would be spared. Caiaphas sought to spare Israel any Roman retribution for harboring a possible insurrectionist; Pilate played the politician and gave Jesus up to satisfy the demands of his constituency. Having acted out their roles of leadership, they would have been dismayed at reports that Jesus had risen from the grave. Pilate would ignore the stories; Caiaphas would start counter rumors of grave robbery.

Nicodemus, while possibly agreeing that a substitution had indeed taken place, might have reflected back on his nighttime conversation with Jesus and concluded that the best of Israel had been murdered by his own national family. Yes, Jesus was a substitute, but not in the way of Caiaphas's and Pilate's thinking. Jesus was a substitute in that he was a representative of all of Israel, and in him all of Israel had died. When stories of the resurrection reached his ears, did he realize that the One who represented the people of God had, indeed, been reborn? The cryptic conversation of John chapter three might now make sense to him.

Peter and the pilgrims in Jerusalem at Pentecost—those who were "cut to the heart"—would recognize the culpability of the people of Israel in the death of Jesus. Whether or not they were in the city when Jesus' death occurred, they were part of the family of God that routinely stoned its prophets. The good news they would all come to know, however, was that in the resurrection—for which death was a prerequisite—"God raised him up, having freed him from death, because it was impossible for him to be held in its power" (Acts 2:24). In Peter's sermon we hear about an unjust act that comes under the *penalty* of sin, yet is forgiven, and also about God's *victory* over death.

Both the Centurion at the cross and the Jewish teacher Gamaliel would speak prophetic words that were expressed in their own observations and reflections about Jesus and the subsequent emergence of the church. The Centurion saw Jesus die and claimed that he must truly be the Son of God. Gamaliel offered his concerned audience the possibility that in the drama of Jesus and the growing band of his followers, God might actually be at work, and to resist him would be futile.

Jesus' friends and family would have moved from deep grief to wonder, and then to a life of mission. The resurrection of Jesus was not, for them, simply a joyous memory, but the launching into God's ongoing work in the world, one for which many of them would die. If there was any sense of *satisfaction* for God, as Peter would attest in his Pentecost sermon, it was that death had been disempowered. The overriding theme for all, including that late arriver Paul, would be one of *victory*—victory over death, over evil, over the principalities and powers that seek to dominate what God seeks to redeem.

There was no one in the story who was not impacted by the death of Jesus. The people were not merely the backdrop to the drama that unfolded in the narrative. The fickle crowds, the Roman executioners, the guards at the tomb, and the pilgrims at Pentecost were not extras on the set, but rather the representation of the world that God so deeply loved

Moving from the Past toward the Future

that, in Jesus Christ, he was doing his incredible work of reconciliation. No one was incidental to the story.

∽

One non-disastrous ground zero is the point of impact of a stone tossed into a pond. From that epicenter ripples form, each diminishing in size and velocity as they radiate outward from the center. As the ripples move the circles get larger, encompassing more space than the original spot where the stone hit the water, yet each successive ripple is oriented around the same center point.

If we think of that day when Jesus died on a Roman cross as a point of impact, then there are ripples that expand outward from that point as more people throughout human history are drawn into the story.[1] As the circles enlarge by both the impact of the event and the passage of time, they remain oriented around that death but continue to move away from it. In the space between the ripples are changes in culture, a shifting in metaphors, new frameworks for understanding complex ideas, and continuous speculation.

The first ripple moving outward from the death of Jesus would have been the experience of those present at the event itself. For them, that ripple was how they saw Jesus' death as an unjust, horrific act; it was the murder of their beloved friend and leader. As the ripple moves outward the perspective widens for these first witnesses, who have experienced Jesus in his resurrection body. While Jesus' death is still interpreted as a travesty, it is then seen in light of God's victory over the power of death. As the ripple moves even further, Jesus is seen as the very embodiment of Israel; he is the one who lives out God's intentions for Israel and simultaneously represents and identifies with his own people.[2] As the ripple

1. Jesus always remains at the epicenter. ". . . Christianity derives its life and meaning from Christ himself. Thus, Christology will always remain central to Christian reflection." Tennent, *Theology in the Context of World Christianity*, 107.

2. The author of the letter to the Hebrews describes Jesus in images associated with the high priesthood of Israel. The high priest represents God to the people through rituals aimed toward forgiveness, and also represents the people to God through the sacrificial system. Jesus, we are told, is the ultimate high priest: ". . . We have such a high priest, one who is seated at the right hand of the throne of the Majesty in the heavens, a minister in the sanctuary and the true tent that the Lord, and not any mortal, has set up." (Heb 8:1–2). James Torrance affirms this double representation both for the high priest of Israel and for Jesus: "When Jesus was born for us at Bethlehem, was baptized by the Spirit in the Jordan, suffered under Pontius Pilate, rose again and ascended, our

continues its progress, Jesus' life, death, resurrection, and continued presence in the world are interpreted as a salvific gift to the entire world.[3] The ripple moves on and it is viewed through the cultural lens of Anselm's feudal England. The lens changes and morphs, and is later exchanged for one that the some of the Reformers would see as something to be interpreted as a judicatory event that set the cosmic scales of justice at balance. And the ripples still continue to move from the original point of impact.

While the dominant atonement images of satisfaction and substitution were crafted in the western world, the ripples are not contained there but instead widen and spread outward, touching new cultures in ever-moving points in history.[4] Each cultural setting attempts to capture the meaning of the atonement in images that are meaningful in a particular historical context.[5] Over time, the images are prone to ossification and can be canonized as the only orthodox way in which the atonement can be expressed. When the metaphors override the meaning, people will eventually crash against them.

Just as the ripples in the pond are not self-created but are results of the stone that has plunged into the water, so the various images of the atonement do not arise out of a vacuum but rather from the historic events of Jesus' entire sojourn on planet earth, the memory of which has

---

humanity was born again, baptized by the Spirit, suffered, died, rose again and ascended in him, in his representative vicarious humanity. Now he presents us in himself to the Father as God's dear children, and our righteousness is hid with Christ in God —ready to be revealed at the last day. Conversely, because Jesus has lived our life, offered himself through the eternal Spirit without spot to the Father in our name and on our behalf, as the one for the many, God accepts us in him. We are accepted in the beloved Son. . ." Torrance, *Worship, Community & the Triune God of Grace*, 49–50.

3. As evidenced by the gift of the Holy Spirit to the Gentiles (Acts 10–11); also Paul's statement in 1 Cor. 5:14–15: "For the love of Christ urges us on, because we are convinced that one has died for all; therefore all have died. And he died for all, so that those who live might live no longer for themselves, but for him who died and was raised for them."

4. It is interesting to note that the Christian faith was birthed in the east, yet the most dominant images of the atonement are grounded in western thought and metaphors.

5. For example, in African theology the focus of the atonement tends toward the model of *Christus Victor*: ". . . A common underlying theme is an emphasis on the power and victory of Christ. All of the major African Christological images, such as Christ as Liberator, Chief, Ancestor, Healer, Master of Initiation, and so on, tend to portray Christ in terms of power as *Christus Victor*." Tennant, *Theology in the Context of World Christianity*, 115. Norman Kraus, in speaking of communicating the atonement in shame-based cultures (e.g., Japan), claims, "*The cross is the epitome of this identification with us in shame.*" Kraus, *Jesus Christ Our Lord*, 217.

Moving from the Past toward the Future

been filtered through the ages by thinkers who have recast the meaning of the atonement within contemporary metaphors.[6] Behind it all, however, is the repetition of the creedal affirmation,

> He was conceived by the power of the Holy Spirit and born of the Virgin Mary. He suffered under Pontius Pilate, was crucified, died, and was buried. He descended to the dead. On the third day he rose again. He ascended into heaven . . .

The earliest Christians were impacted deeply by the death of Jesus, and as the New Testament witnesses have shown, their responses ranged from grief, to outrage, to accusations of murder, and even wonder. It was the resurrection that focused their attention on what God was doing, and the subsequent work of the Holy Spirit, as described in the Acts of the Apostles, drew them into a new story of life and mission that framed their newly-formed communities of faith. Until the arrival of Paul, little theological interpretation of Jesus' death was offered.

It was inevitable, however, that such interpretation would be necessary. In the increasing awareness of God's unique presence in the person of Jesus, Christian thinkers would struggle with the idea that God's work of reconstituting the people of God and reconciling the world to himself in and through Jesus had to include a grisly death on a Roman cross. Throughout the ages, Christians have seen saving significance in the death of Jesus, and to exclude his death from a theology of the atonement is as costly as dismissing the incarnation or the resurrection. It is all part of the story of God's redeeming work in the world.

The question must be asked: What really happens if the death of Jesus on the cross ceases to be the *single* motif by which the atonement is understood and articulated? If our concept of the atonement changes so that the death of Jesus is no longer seen as a physical enactment that contains in itself all that God has done on behalf of the world, but rather

---

6. Christopher Wright recognizes the reality and benefit of biblical interpretation through various historical and cultural lenses: "Even when we affirm (as I certainly do) that the historical and salvation-historical context of biblical texts and their authors is of primary and objective importance in discerning their meaning and their significance, the plurality of perspectives from which readers read them is also a vital factor in the hermeneutical richness of the global church. What persons of one culture bring from that culture to their reading of a text may illuminate dimensions or implications of the text itself that persons of another culture may have not seen so clearly." Wright, *The Mission of God*, 39.

as a much more complex and mysterious reality, have we abandoned the faith? Is something lost if that happens?

The answer is *no*: we have not abandoned the faith. But the answer is also *yes*: we do lose something. We lose a monochromatic portrait of what God has done for the world in and through Jesus Christ. We lose a fixation on the supposed transactional nature of Jesus' death that obscures the incredible significance of the incarnation, the resurrection, the unleashing of the Holy Spirit, and the commissioning of God's people to participate in his mission of reconciliation of the world. We lose the perceived safety of a cognitive affirmation of honorific or judicial absolution that we can confidently describe as *orthodox*. There is a lot to lose.

But there is also much to gain. By looking at the whole story of Jesus, we gain a broad embrace of what it means, that ". . . in Christ, God was reconciling the world to himself, not counting their trespasses against them" (2 Cor 5:19). We gain a refreshed posture of worship in recognizing that, in the incarnation, God has given himself fully to the world in Jesus Christ, who, in the complete experience of real human life, ". . . in every respect has been tested as we are, yet without sin" (Heb 4:15b). We gain the realization that we, like the first friends of Jesus, are not concretized into a theological framework, but rather are catapulted into God's ongoing mission in the world.

At the same time, we dare not lose the significance of Jesus' death. In spite of the many possible interpretations of the meaning of that death, it cannot be reduced to a comma in the manuscript of Christian faith—the Bible will not allow us that reduction. The Bible speaks of Jesus' death as something *real*—an event at a particular time in human history that has to do with God's universal mission in the world. What the Bible does allow is a multiplicity of lenses through which we view that death.

Looking at the death of Jesus with new eyes need not deny the significance of the cross, even while challenging the pathways that various culturally-based traditions have taken in regards to the atonement. New ways of looking at the death of Jesus vary in both scope and validity, but such theological reflection has been taking place since the earliest days of the church.

As a contemporary example, Brian McLaren raises the lens of nonviolence and examines what has happened in Jesus' willingness to go to the cross:

Moving from the Past toward the Future

> After praying "Your will be done" in the Garden of Gethsemane, after choosing self-sacrifice over self-protection, he walked like a lamb into the middle of the forest, so the wolves would come out of the shadow and circle around him. Then he stretched out his neck, as it were, inviting them to pounce, and they did. Ironically, though, as he exposed his own neck, he also exposed their vicious wolfishness, and in that way he sabotaged them, defeated them, rendering them ugly and incredible. After all, they could no longer claim to be agents of peace and promise after torturing and killing a good and peaceful man so violently and shamefully.[7]

In a generous critique of McLaren's view, Scot McKnight challenges an interpretation of Jesus' death that focuses strictly on the upending of violence and injustice:

> The most stable location for the earliest understandings of the Cross, from Jesus all the way through the New Testament writings, is the Last Supper—and not a word is said there about violence and systemic injustice. Other words are given to explain the event: *covenant*, *forgiveness of sins*, and *blood* "poured out for many." Insight into the Cross must start here. In fact, I question whether a cross that only undoes violence is enough to create liberation, peace, and a kingdom vision.[8]

And so the conversation continues (hopefully, with the kind of civility expressed in the above exchange), pushing and pulling in different but related directions. Are we able to embrace a broad, multi-faceted view of the atonement without forfeiting the significance of the death of Jesus?[9] Is there a way for us to remain both true to our scriptural narrative and open to multiple perspectives? Is the way that we communicate the atonement important to the lives of people who hear the message? As Carroll and Green point out, we face a dilemma when it comes to understanding and communicating the significance of the cross:

---

7. McLaren, *Everything Must Change*, 272.
8. McKnight, "McLaren Emerging," *Christianity Today*,
9. Weaver points out that some feminist theologians, finding traditional views of the atonement (interpreted as the Father sacrificing the Son) to be tantamount to cosmic child abuse, would discard atonement theology altogether. Certain feminist theologians ". . . do not articulate a comprehensive atonement formula as a foundation for Christian faith that avoids the problems of an image of abuse. In fact, they believe that atonement theology must be jettisoned." Weaver, *The Nonviolent Atonement*, 130.

> First, today we must grapple with appropriating language suitable to communicating the profundity of Jesus' salvific work to people outside the Christian faith as well as those inside the church. Second, we must do so in a way that does justice to the biblical presentation of the work of Jesus. This means, first and foremost, that the cross can never be neglected or marginalized in Christian proclamation, given the centrality of the cross to the writings of the NT.[10]

The cross still stands at ground zero, symbolizing for us the full spectrum of what God has done in and through Jesus. While the Gospels and Acts offer accounts of what happened on the day that Jesus died and generally avoid articulating systematic statements that interpret the meaning of his death, the narratives are permeated with suggestions that Jesus died *for us*. The apostle Paul affirms this understanding as part of the earliest tradition of the church:

> For I handed on to you as of first importance what I in turn had received: that Christ died for our sins in accordance with the Scriptures . . . (1 Cor 15:3)

What God has done includes the whole of Jesus' conception, birth, life, suffering, death, resurrection, and ascension. Yet Jesus' death stands as a pivot point between the existence he has shared with us and the life that is yet to come.[11] His death on the cross is not the entirety of the atonement, but there is no doubt that the Scriptures point to the saving significance of his death. We turn to that significance now.

---

10. Carroll and Green, *The Death of Jesus in Early Christianity*, 275.

11. Hence the apostle Paul's interpretation of the gospel as both the death and resurrection of Jesus. As Daniel Kirk observes, "Both 1 Cor 15:1–4 and Gal 3:1–18 corroborate the notion that Paul thinks of the gospel in terms of what God has done in the death and resurrection of Jesus, and that this work corresponds to what is written in the Scriptures of Israel." Kirk, *Unlocking Romans*, 45 n56.

11

The Death of Jesus and God's Self-Giving Love

> Through him God was pleased to reconcile to himself all things, whether on earth or in heaven, by making peace through the blood of his cross. (Col 1:20)

> . . . How extraordinary it is that our lives have been redeemed, literally made possible, by the life, death, and resurrection of Jesus Christ.[1]

> The beginning of atonement is the sense of its necessity.[2]

IT SHOULD BE NO mystery that human beings are drawn to the idea of atonement. After all, it would be the rare person who would not agree that there is something wrong with the world and, by association, with all people. As Christian thinkers throughout the ages have wrestled with atonement theory, the looming realities of evil, guilt, and shame have demanded their attention. Various cultures have sought to appease their deities with sacrifices and rituals; Christians have tried to understand how it is that Jesus takes care of everything for us. In this book I have

---

1. Stanley Hauerwas, *Cross-Shattered Christ*, 21.
2. Lord Byron, http://www.brainyquote.com/quotes/keywords/atonement.html. Accessed 1/15/12.

tried to explore that understanding primarily through the experiences of those present at or near the time of Jesus' death.

None of those present at the ground zero of Jesus' crucifixion would have divorced him from the life that led to the cross. His death was not an isolated theological event but rather an explosive, mind-numbing experience that translated quickly into joy, hope, and mission. Even those who did not know Jesus before the crucifixion—such as many among the gathered crowds and the executioners—would have seen a real, live human being dragged to the cross and nailed down like a wind-blown shutter. For all present, Jesus' death was tied intimately to his life.

During a class session in systematic theology, my seminary professor—a man not shy about stirring up controversy—asked the question, "If, in the garden of Gethsemane, under the great stress of anticipating his impending arrest and crucifixion, Jesus died of a heart attack, would he have died for our sins?" I didn't immediately know how to answer his question, but I expected a lively and spirited class discussion to explode any second. I was not disappointed.

My professor was not attempting to disparage the reality of the cross. Rather, he was attempting to get us to think about the implications of the incarnation. If, indeed, in Jesus the fullness of God dwelt (Col 1:19); if, indeed, Jesus is the Word made flesh (John 1:14), then God has done something in and through the entirety of Jesus' existence on earth that defies complete and full comprehension. The cross is not God's cosmic gamble, his hope-against-hope that Jesus doesn't miss his opportunity for crucifixion; the cross is the *penultimate* event in the life of the one who became "... like his brothers and sisters in every respect" (Heb 2:17a), yet an event that was *ultimately* turned on its head by Jesus' resurrection. As Norman Kraus observes,

> The cross has become the special event and symbol of God's solidarity with us in our sinful existence and his atoning love for humankind. But we must understand that the cross is the consummation of the incarnation itself. The Apostles' Creed sums up the incarnation with the words 'born,' 'suffered,' dead and buried,' and this clearly follows the lead of Paul in his letter to the Philippians (2:5–11). The cross as a discrete act or event cannot be separated from the whole of Jesus' life as though it contained a separate meaning in and of itself. Rather it is an integral, completing part of the whole revelatory incarnation event. *Thus to be precise we*

> *should say that God is justified by an incarnation which finds its consummation in the cross, and not be a legal transaction which took place on a cross.*[3]

While the separating of Jesus' crucifixion from the full story of his preceding life and subsequent resurrection is faulty theology, it would be no less faulty to treat his death as an event that was incidental because of its human inevitability. We are helped when we remember that we are not asked to come to grips with the man Jesus who is sacrificed by God for the purpose of God's satisfaction, but rather with the Son . . . "whom [God] appointed heir of all things, through whom he also created the worlds. He is the reflection of God's glory and the exact imprint of God's very being" (Heb 1:2b-3a).

Atonement theory stumbles when it separates the Father from the Son and pits them against each other in a tragic and violent relationship of appeasement. When the Son becomes a perfect, sacrificial *other* who brings satisfaction to the transcendent God who demands such a requirement, then our understanding of the depth of relationship that is shared by the Father and Son suffers from abuse. While the relationship of the eternal Father to the suffering and dying Son raises questions about the nature of God, creating a chasm between the Father and Son that is bridged only by the Son's death is a solution grounded more in the concept of blind western justice than in the doctrine of the Trinity.

The Christian concept of God as Father, Son, and Holy Spirit is of oneness in an eternal relationship of love. While there is an otherness to Jesus as the one who fully identifies with the entire spectrum of human existence, it is an otherness that remains in deep relationship with the Father. As Thomas Torrance points out,

> The fact that Jesus Christ is God's beloved Son means that in him the Father was actively and personally present in the crucifixion of Christ, intervening redemptively in our lostness and darkness. In giving his beloved Son in atoning sacrifice for our sin God has given himself to us in unreserved love, so that the cross is not only a revelation of the love of Christ but a revelation of the love of God. The cross was a window into the very heart of God, for in and behind the cross, it was God the Father himself who paid the cost of our salvation. And so through the shedding of the blood of

---

3. Kraus, *Jesus Christ Our Lord*, 157.

> Christ in atoning sacrifice for our sin the innermost nature of God the Father as holy compassionate love has been revealed to us.[4]

At ground zero, however, would the first witnesses have translated this tragic, violent death so quickly into an expression of God's love for the world, or is this theology of love one that was created to make sense of it all? The four Gospels do not offer such a theology in the accounts of the crucifixion and resurrection (although, in John 21 Jesus does call Peter to new depths of love), but a theology grounded in God's love is clearly expressed by John in the account of the hours spent with Jesus and his friends just prior to his arrest.

John 13–17 offers a glimpse into Jesus' relationship with his disciples that is unique among the four Gospel accounts.[5] The profound and intimate nature of their friendship is revealed as Jesus speaks about love in ways that would surely have impacted the way they would come to understand what God was doing in the death of Jesus.

John places Jesus and his disciples in a secluded room just prior to Passover where they share a meal. At one point they appear to leave the room (John 14:31b) and head toward the garden where Jesus will be arrested. All the while, Jesus speaks to them, and the most dominant theme is love:

> Now before the festival of the Passover, Jesus knew that his hour had come to depart from this world and go to the Father. Having loved his own who were in the world, he loved them to the end. (John 13:1)

There is something sorrowful about this scene. Jesus knows that death is coming and his love for his friends is not incidental to what is happening. We know from the Gospel accounts the grief suffered by Jesus' followers when he died, but this text provides a glimpse into the pain of love that Jesus experienced as he prepared to leave his companions. The picture that John has crafted is not one in which love is an abstract theological concept, but rather one that is deeply personal, grounded in the shared life that has bonded these men together.

---

4. Torrance, *The Mediation of Christ*, 109.

5. Thompson cautions that the uniqueness of John's account should not be severed from history: "While John's Gospel is often labeled the most theological or the most interpretative—characterizations often understood as equivalent—of the four Gospels, John's creativity operates within definite limits, and his theological reflections remain tethered to historical realities." Thompson, *The God of the Gospel of John*, 236.

The Death of Jesus and God's Self-Giving Love

Scholars affirm that all the Gospels were written decades after the events they describe.[6] By the time of John's writing, he was confident enough in the identification of Jesus with God the Father to convey these words of Jesus:

> "Whoever has seen me has seen the Father." (John 14:9)

This Jesus who sits before his disciples is not one who is detached from God and turned loose to suffer a prophet's fate in a violent world. In all that his friends have seen in him—his presence, his character, his words, his miracles—the face of God has been revealed.[7] Jesus' words of love come as a gift from God, drawing the disciples together in love for one another, but also enveloping them in the oneness of love that Jesus shares with the Father. Jesus would affirm that in prayer:

> The glory that you have given me I have given them, so that they may be one, as we are one, I in them and you in me, that they may become completely one, so that the world may know that you have sent me and have loved them even as you have loved me. (John 16:22–23)

If words such as these were truly spoken by Jesus to his friends prior to his death,[8] then the disciples would eventually have to come to grips with the idea that all that had happened—including Jesus' death—was somehow wrapped up in God's love for both Jesus and them. It is unlikely that they connected the dots immediately—tragedy and grief don't usually allow for that kind of interpretive speed—but instead saw the linkages emerge as they lived out the post-resurrection life of mission and love.

If the synoptic Gospels and Acts were the only witnesses we had to the story of Jesus, it might be easy to see the role of Christians to be somewhat utilitarian. Matthew, Mark, and Luke-Acts all convey a commissioning from Jesus to his disciples (Matt 28:18–20, Mark 16:15, Luke 24:44–48,

---

6. Most scholars suggest a range of thirty-five to sixty-five years after Jesus' death.

7. "... The Gospel [of John] has made it clear that the identity of Jesus cannot be fully comprehended unless grasped as the manifestation and revelation of God." Thompson, *The God of the Gospel of John*, 235.

8. Marshall expresses confidence in the Johannine conversations. He sees the gospels as four perspectives of the same theological framework, but still gives John a unique place among the accounts: "The Synoptic Gospels are probably much closer to the *ipsissima verba* of Jesus and to his teaching about the future, whereas the Johannine literature evidences a much more developed theology that reflects more fully the insights of early Christians in the period after the resurrection." Marshall, *New Testament Theology*, 593.

Acts 1:8), certainly one that carries the promise of the Holy Spirit, but also clearly focused on participation in God's mission in the world. It is John who frames the shared and missional life of the emerging church in love. As he[9] would write to some struggling Christian communities:

> God's love was revealed among us in this way: God sent his only Son into the world so that we might live through him. In this is love, not that we loved God but that he loved us and sent his Son to be the atoning sacrifice for our sins. Beloved, since God loved us so much, we also ought to love one another. No one has ever seen God; if we love one another, God lives in us, and his love is perfected in us. (1 John 4:9–12)

It is unlikely that this theme of love was foreign to the disciples' understanding of Jesus and somehow appeared spontaneously in the writings of John many years after the crucifixion and resurrection. While Jesus' monologue about love and oneness is captured in John 13–17, it can be assumed that these themes permeated his interactions with his followers during his three years with them. As their thinking about the Son's relationship to the Father developed, the disciples would surely have seen something startling in Jesus' comment about God ("Whoever has seen me has seen the Father") and the nature of self-sacrificing love:

> No one has greater love than this, to lay down one's life for one's friends. (John 15:13)

After the resurrection, the disciples would not forget the intimate relationship between Jesus and his heavenly Father. The God of Israel proved himself to be fully invested in his people—and the world—through all that had happened. God's full participation in and identification with the life, suffering, death, and resurrection of Jesus would be revealed beyond the small band of followers when Peter would proclaim on the day of Pentecost,

> "Repent, and be baptized every one of you in the name of Jesus Christ so that your sins may be forgiven; and you will receive the gift of the Holy Spirit. For the promise is for you, for your children, and for all who are far away, everyone whom the Lord our God calls to him." (Acts 2:38–39)

---

9. Most scholars affirm the common authorship of the fourth Gospel and the epistles of John. See G. M. Burge, "*John, Letters of*," 595.

The Death of Jesus and God's Self-Giving Love

The God who was reflected in the person of Jesus, the God who raised Jesus from the dead, was the God of promise to his people. This was no vindictive deity; this was the God who forgave sins, just as Jesus had prayed from the cross on behalf of his murderers. In addition, this God would make good on Jesus' prayer for oneness and pour out the presence of the Holy Spirit into the lives of those who turned to him. This was love as it was meant to be experienced: Self-sacrificing, forgiving, inviting, and fully present. It was as Jesus described:

> "Those who love me will keep my word, and my Father will love them, and we will come to them and make our home with them." (John 14:23)

At the moment of his death, those gathered at the foot of the cross would have seen, in that ravaged and lifeless body, not only the man Jesus, but the Father with whom he was one.[10] That the oneness of the Father with the Son would be so fully identified with the world that suffering and death would not be side-stepped revealed something shocking to the faithful mourners: The salvation that was offered to Israel and the world came not from the God who put the weight on the back of the innocent, but instead came from the self-sacrificing God of love who was willing to endure a human death.

---

10. Goldingay connects Jesus' death with God's (Yhwh) self-sacrificing relationship to Israel: "Given the definition of divinity (or rather, of the distinctive divine nature of Yhwh) in the First Testament, submitting to execution is actually an expression of Jesus' sharing in the identity of Yhwh as the compassionate God who would go to the uttermost lengths for Israel but will not compromise over right and wrong. Yhwh has been submitting to death through the First Testament story, persisting in the relationship that continually involved rejection and hurt, yet without ceasing to stand up for what is right. Yhwh has been paying the penalty for utilizing Israel in seeking to implement a plan to restore the world to what it was meant to be. Yhwh has been bearing the cost of a relationship with Israel. Jesus' execution is the logical conclusion to that story of paying the penalty and bearing the cost of the world's restoration." (Goldingay, *Old Testament Theology: Israel's Gospel*, 830.

12

At the Margins of Ground Zero: Preaching the Atonement

> Now when Jesus had finished saying these things, the crowds were astounded at his teaching, for he taught them as one having authority, and not as their scribes. (Matt 7:28–29)

> ... We are ambassadors for Christ, since God is making his appeal through us; we entreat you on behalf of Christ, be reconciled to God. For our sake he made him to be sin who knew no sin, so that in him we might become the righteousness of God. (2 Cor 5:20–21)

> The human race has been in exile; exiled from the garden, shut out of the house, bombarded with noise instead of music. Our task is to announce in deed and word that the exile is over, to enact the symbols that speak of healing and forgiveness, to act boldly in the power of the Spirit.[1]

WALTER BRUEGGEMANN STUNS OUR sensibilities when he claims that we, as American Christians, are a people in exile. We tend to view ourselves as free and privileged (at least in contrast to other societies), not as oppressed and captive. Brueggemann, however, argues that our exile is not defined in terms of geographical banishment or physical enslavement,

---

1. Wright, *The Challenge of Easter*, 46–47.

At the Margins of Ground Zero: Preaching the Atonement

but rather in terms of the exchange of our faith tradition for the perceived benefits of a material society:

> The contemporary American church is so largely enculturated to the American ethos of consumerism that it has little power to believe or to act. This enculturation is in some way true across the spectrum of church life, both liberal and conservative. It may not be a new situation, but it is one that seems especially urgent and pressing at the present time. That enculturation is true not only of the institution of the church but also of us as persons. Our consciousness has been claimed by false fields of perception and idolatrous systems of language and rhetoric.[2]

Of course, this type of exile is not limited to Americans in the United States. Any culture that has embraced consumerism as a core value and an economic necessity will be scandalized by the suggestion that all members of that culture—including Christians—have been so deeply imprinted that the prophetic word becomes offensive when heard. Yet the prophetic word that preaches atonement is one that runs counter to the word of the dominant consumer culture that offers happiness with the swipe of a credit card.[3] Atonement preached brings liberation and life rather than enslavement to debt-ridden economic and social value systems. Brueggemann likens the ancient Hebrew prophets to lyricists who produce music of hope that points to an alternative reality:

> The poet in exile sings his people to homecoming. And that is a theme to which the exiled church in America is now summoned. The gospel is that we may go home. Home is not here in the consumer militarism of a dominant value system. Home also is not in heaven, as though we may escape. Home, rather is God's kingdom of love and justice and peace and freedom that waits for us. The news is we are invited home (cf. Luke 15:17). The whole church may yet sing: "precious Saviour take my hand. Lead me home!"[4]

The message of atonement is not, of course, addressed only to the bondage of consumerism. People throughout the world—both Christian and otherwise—find themselves locked in cages of oppression, guilt, shame, and brokenness that can only be unlocked by the good news of what God has done in and through Jesus Christ. The healing that comes

---

2. Brueggemann, *The Prophetic Imagination*, 11.
3. Or in the ruling power of dictatorial tyrants that too many nations still endure.
4. Brueggemann, *Hopeful Imagination*, 130.

is not a function of the transfer of theological information, but rather an invitation into the grand, transforming story that gives meaning to all other stories and draws the hearer into a new life that is defined by the life, suffering, death, and resurrection of Jesus rather than by other stories that demand allegiance.

How the atonement is communicated in preaching, teaching, and conversation is not incidental to the life of the church or to its mission in the world. Atonement is not an abstract theological concept that belongs only under "A" in a dusty theological dictionary. Atonement is about God, and it draws all hearers into the possibility of new life in and through Jesus. Communicating the atonement is crucial for the church, both as hearers and as proclaimers. This is about more than simple methodology; it is about immersion in the multi-faceted images and metaphors that Scripture provides and our willingness to recognize our own limited insight into the mysterious and wonderful work of God for the world.

How the atonement is heard is crucial for the church. If atonement is communicated only in terms of western concepts of guilt, will shame go unaddressed? If it is framed in proclamations of victory that guarantee success and prosperity in life, will the poor, oppressed, and broken among us be relegated to the margins of faith? What God has done for the world is a story so rich and expansive that it reaches out to all people in all times and cultures. It speaks not only to our inner lives but also to our interpersonal relationships, our ethics, and our politics.

If atonement is about the fullness and entirety of God in Jesus Christ, then the story speaks into our perceptions about the character of God and draws us into a transformed life and a story that is more expansive than we've ever imagined:

- *Atonement is about incarnation.* That God, in Jesus, would enter fully into human existence tells us that God is both transcendent and immanent; that he doesn't demand that we climb a mountain to find him because, in Jesus, he has already found us.

- *Atonement is about life.* This God-life-in-Christ was lived not only in the dramas of the Gospels, but also in the unwritten rhythms of Jesus in his eating, sleeping, working, and playing. In Jesus, God is present in the high drama as well as in the ordinariness of our lives.

- *Atonement is about suffering.* In the sufferings of Jesus, God identifies with human pain and anguish. Those who suffer are no longer pushed to the margins of righteousness, but instead are drawn to the center of God's care and compassion.

- *Atonement is about death.* As Jesus dies, he identifies his life with that of Israel and ultimately, the world. God-in-Christ allows death to exert its power—a death orchestrated and fueled by the sin of God's own people—and God's identification with the world completes the full cycle of human existence. In the death of Jesus, God is truly seen as *Emmanuel*—God is with us.

- *Atonement is about the grave.* His lifeless body prone and wrapped in grave clothes, Jesus lies alongside all human beings who have died or will one day die. God-in-Christ does not turn his back on the grave, but instead enters the place of death with us, giving us hope for new life. With the psalmist we can rejoice,

  For you do not give me up to Sheol, or let your faithful one see the Pit. (Ps 16:10)

- *Atonement is about resurrection.* When the bonds of the tomb are exploded as God raises Jesus from the dead, death's grip on the fears of humanity is also broken. The screeching cheers of sin are silenced as the truth about sin is revealed: It no longer is the inevitable definer of human life. In Jesus, death no longer has the last word; it is God who now holds the floor and says,

  "See, I am making all things new." (Rev 21:5a)

- *Atonement is about ascension.* Jesus ascends to the presence of the Father, and in doing so establishes the victory of God over sin, death, principalities, and powers, and declares the supremacy of his reign over all others. In that victory we find freedom from all that seeks to occupy and oppress us—all that is not God.

- *Atonement is about the Holy Spirit.* Atonement defies the reductionism of a cosmic transaction that guarantees a ticket on the bus to heaven. In the outpouring of the Holy Spirit, the very breath of God reanimates those who have trusted in Jesus, drawing them into a new, dynamic life and full participation in God's mission in the world. We are not pardoned by the cosmic judge who has no further interest in us once we are forgiven. Instead, the forgiven ones are

- *Atonement is about the Kingdom of God.* What God has done in and through Jesus is not simply to create a safe passage to heaven for you and me. Forgiveness of sins includes both pardon and liberation from the consequences of exile. Our liberation is found in the gift of the Holy Spirit and also our new citizenship in God's reign. All the powers of sin and death cannot compete with God's kingdom because the cross and the empty tomb have disempowered them. As the apostle Paul declared,

fully embraced by the Father who calls us home again, to give ourselves to the life that is God's mission of love.

> The last enemy to be destroyed is death. (1 Cor 15:26)

~

Those who preach have been assaulted by distractions over the years. We are distracted by the need to grow our churches, and preaching about the felt needs of self-esteem, finances, marriage, and the pursuit of happiness has become the preferred way of reaching new people. Fears about the direction of the nation have caused some to preach against perceived political and social foes. Desires to offer church services in culturally relevant ways have created burdens of high, costly productions and the never-ending search for that *cutting edge*. John Wright's critique is insightful:

> Each sermon must fulfill the expectations of the congregation—expectations usually formed by the consumerist, entertainment-oriented society we live in. Clergy have instinctively responded to the situation. . . . The serious engagement of the biblical text itself becomes shaped by accommodation to the contemporary world. The concern for daily living can easily overwhelm the voice of the biblical text, except in the faint echo of biblical citations.[5]

While all the concerns about meeting people in their places of need, addressing global issues, and framing the worship expressions of the church with a sensitivity to cultural relevance are not unimportant, they are not the heart of our message. The heart of our message is God-in-Christ. Robert Farrar Capon describes how the focus on the work that God has done in and through Jesus frees the preacher from such distractions:

---

5. Wright, *Telling God's Story*, 17.

At the Margins of Ground Zero: Preaching the Atonement

> . . . The most passionately wonderful thing about it is the way it delivers you, as a preacher, from having to spout uplifting hokum from the pulpit. No useless programs of life improvement need ever pass your lips; no empty threats about what will happen to your people if they don't improve will ever insult their intelligence, or yours. You won't have to tell them that love will make their lives soar upward like eagles, if only they'll work harder at it. That's a lie. . . . You won't have to warn them that they must stop sinning if they want God to like them. That's another lie. . . . Above all, you won't even have to tell them they need to be morally upright to earn God's favor. That's the biggest, bad-news lie of all, because God has gone and accepted every last one of them in his beloved Son and is as pleased as punch with them in Jesus. If you can make up your mind, when you go into the pulpit, to forget everything except Jesus Christ and him crucified, you'll have nothing to give them but *Good News*.[6]

If the focal point of preaching is the therapeutic needs of people, then we enter dangerous territory; preaching as therapy in an individualistic, consumeristic culture is a very slippery slope. That is not to say that the hearers do not require a therapeutic touch, if by that we mean that they need to be healed from the many things that can damage, distort, and injure the bodies, hearts, and minds of human beings.[7] But if the focus of preaching is Jesus and the story that God is writing in the world, then the opportunity emerges for all personal stories to find meaning and healing in that grand narrative.[8] In preaching the atonement, we cannot avoid drawing people into the biblical narrative that is permeated by a variety of metaphors while at the same time experiencing the need for new metaphors to arise.

Getting comfortable with the limitation of metaphor is no small task. Many western Christians have become so ingrained with the metaphors associated with penal substitution that suggestions about other images of the atonement are often viewed with suspicion if not outrage. The work of the biblical preacher involves faithfulness to the Scriptures, but it also

---

6. Capon, *The Foolishness of Preaching*, 12–13.

7. We get our word *therapy* from the Greek word *therapeusai*, which is translated in the New Testament as *to heal* (for example, see Luke 14:3).

8. "The question is not, How can we make the Scriptures relevant to individuals in need of therapy? but, How do we translate human lives into the biblical narrative to live as part of the body of Christ in the world?" Wright, *Telling God's Story*, 19.

demands that our texts be interpreted so that each generation can hear. Mark Baker points out the tension that is required for such preaching:

> If we would be faithful to Scripture, we too must continuously seek out metaphors, new and old, that speak effectively and specifically to our various worlds. Yet, if we would follow in the path of the New Testament writers, the metaphors we deploy would be at home in our settings, but never too comfortable here. Those writers sought, and urge us to seek, not only to be understood by people and social systems around us, but also to shape them. Moreover, we would not eschew earlier models or the reality to which they point, but would carry on our constructive work fully in conversation with and under the guidance of the Scriptures of Israel and the church, and of apostolic testimony.[9]

Revisiting the atonement at the epicenter of ground zero helps both the preacher and the hearer to hold loosely to culturally-determined metaphors and to engage deeply with the narrative that has birthed those metaphors. In allowing our imaginations to join the first witnesses to Jesus' death and finding ourselves cringing at the pounding of the nails, running in fear of being discovered, missing the point and committing an act of betrayal, weeping tears of grief, and experiencing resurrection joy and wonder, we can explore the metaphors of atonement and find our own stories there.

My hope in this book is that, by engaging our minds and imaginations in the narratives of the Gospels and Acts, and exploring the impact that the death of Jesus might have had on the first witnesses to that historic event, we would come to consider two things: First, that the significance of the death of Jesus does not begin with any particular theory of the atonement, but rather with the reality as we see it reflected in the Apostles' Creed:

> He suffered under Pontius Pilate, was crucified, died, and was buried.

From that real beginning of suffering and death, Christian thinkers throughout the ages have attempted to interpret that death theologically, and many cultural frameworks and metaphors—some from Scripture, some not—have been employed in those endeavors. Those frameworks

---

9. Baker, *Proclaiming the Scandal of the Cross*, 18.

and metaphors are important to the extent that they help people in particular times and places to find meaning in the atonement both theologically and personally. The frameworks and metaphors become problematic when they become concretized in our imaginations so that no other way of thinking about the atonement is allowed.

I have also argued that atonement is not limited to Jesus' death, but embraces the entirety of what God has done in Jesus Christ through his conception, life, suffering, death, resurrection, and ascension. The atonement results not only in a spiritual transformation that can be translated theologically, but (according to our Scriptures) also in the empowerment by the Holy Spirit and the emergence of the church, both of which provide demonstrations of the present reality of the kingdom of God and God's mission in the world.

For most Christians, an understanding of the atonement will come through the hearing of a message, typically in the form of a sermon.[10] The preacher stands before the people with a difficult and wonderful task, to speak clearly and prophetically the word of the Lord as it comes to us through Scripture and by the work of the Holy Spirit. Preaching must be clear in the sense that all effective communication must be clear in order to be cognitively grasped by the hearers. But it also must be clear in its portrayal of the narrative that is Scripture. In other words, the story must be told well and the telling must be faithful to the text. The word must also be spoken prophetically, not in the more popular sense of seeing the future, but as a word that draws people away from the demands of the dominant culture and into the desires and intentions of God for his people, and ultimately for the world.

In speaking of the lives of the ancient Hebrew prophets of the Bible, Abraham Heschel speaks of the complexity of prophetic work:

> The prophet's task is to convey a divine view, yet as a person he *is* a point of view. He speaks from the perspective of God as perceived from the perspective of his own situation. We must seek to understand not only the views he expounded but also the attitudes he embodied: his own position, feeling, response—not only what he said but also what he lived. . .[11]

---

10. And reinforced by hymns and other musical lyrics.
11. Heschel, *The Prophets*, xxii.

Atonement at Ground Zero

The prophetic word does not emerge from a vacuum, but comes as a gift of the Spirit and passes through the life and cultural grids that form both the preacher and the people. How we speak in a way that is simultaneously true to our biblical narrative, humble about our own limitations of understanding, open to the move of the Holy Spirit, and pastoral in how we help people to orient their lives in the alternate reality of God's kingdom is crucial to prophetic preaching. It is also a daunting task.

Most of us who preach have been apprenticed along the way by those who have devoted themselves to the art and practice of preaching. There are many fine resources available, ranging from the traditional to the ones that seek to push the envelope of preaching to new and unexplored dimensions. Books that have helped me along the way include Thomas Long's *The Witness of Preaching*, Robert Farrar Capon's *The Foolishness of Preaching*, Barbara Brown Taylor's *Preaching Life*, Doug Pagitt's *Preaching in the Inventive Age* (formerly published as *Preaching Re-Imagined*) and John Wright's fine book, *Telling God's Story*. In my own crafting of sermons over the years, the fingerprints of these helpers are often found on the pages.

But it is not the fingerprints of writers on preaching that matter in the end. What impacts the hearers most significantly is, metaphorically, to grab the manuscript from the preacher's hand and, like good prophetic detectives, dust for the fingerprints of God. While a word spoken in a particular context with relevant cultural images is important for the sake of intelligibility, it is the voice of God that needs to be heard. The preacher stands in a posture of fear and trembling as the task of preaching is undertaken.

Fear and trembling are prerequisites for preaching the atonement. The depth, complexity, and mystery of what God has done in and through Jesus Christ for the sake of the world demands a communicative task that cannot be limited to mere cognitive affirmation, but must be realized and lived out in the daily lives of the people who comprise the body of Christ. As John Wright insists:

> It is extremely important that the Christian life not be left as an abstraction; it is life within a concrete people, witnessing to God's intent for all creation as we await God's kingdom to come on earth as it is in heaven.[12]

---
12. Wright, *Telling God's Story*, 101.

At the Margins of Ground Zero: Preaching the Atonement

It with fear and trembling that I offer some of my own sermons that focus on the atonement, as clearly and faithfully as I am able, from the perspective of ground zero.[13] I do not include these messages because they represent examples of the best exegetical and homiletic practices—there are many fine resources available that will do a much better job at those things than I am able. They do, however, offer how I have processed the reality and meaning of the atonement for myself and then attempted to communicate that unfolding perception to others in my pastoral care.

THE LAST WORDS OF JESUS: "MY GOD, MY GOD, WHY HAVE YOU FORSAKEN ME?"

This short homily was given on April 6, 2007, at St. James Anglican Church in Newport Beach, California. Seven speakers were invited to preach on one of the seven last utterances of Jesus as he died on the cross.

∼

> When it was noon, darkness came over the whole land until three in the afternoon. At three o'clock Jesus cried out with a loud voice, "Eloi, Eloi, lema sabachthani?" which means, "My God, my God, why have you forsaken me?" (Mark 15:33–34)

One of the deepest human fears is the fear of abandonment. To be left isolated, unguarded, vulnerable to the whims of the universe is the ultimate form of fear and loneliness.

When we imagine Jesus hanging from that Roman cross, crying out in apparent desperation, his cry, "Why have you forsaken me?" touches on our own fears. If God could forsake one so innocent as Jesus, why would he not forsake me, if even for a day?

Jesus is truly alone on the cross. Yes, there are people standing about, watching, grieving, mocking—yet he bears the pain and suffering by himself. And he bears it all, it seems, even without the One he has intimately called *Abba, Father*.

It is interesting that the Gospel writer makes a point of letting us know the time frame of the darkness that came over the land: From noon

---

13. For a helpful collection of messages that offer new ways to communicate the atonement, see Mark D. Baker, *Proclaiming the Scandal of the Cross: Contemporary Images of the Atonement*.

until three. It was really a significant time of day for the Jewish community. Noon would be the midday break from the day's labors and a time for communal prayer. Many would find rest after that, concluding the break around three in the afternoon—the ninth hour, as they would call it—with another time of prayer.

Noon to three was a time frame bracketed by prayer. When we look closely at Jesus' last words we realize that Jesus joined his own praying community by crying out words that were not a random scream of terror but rather the opening words of the familiar prayer of Psalm 22. Jesus, in quoting these lines, brings an invitation to enter fully into the larger prayer of the psalm:

> My God, my God, why have you forsaken me? Why are you so far from helping me, from the words of my groaning? O my God, I cry by day, but you do not answer; and by night, but find no rest. Yet you are holy, enthroned on the praises of Israel. In you our ancestors trusted; they trusted, and you delivered them. To you they cried, and were saved; in you they trusted, and were not put to shame. (Ps 22:1–5)

The prayer of Psalm 22 goes on to describe a person's experience of desperation and pain. The description of suffering sounds strangely like the agony of one being crucified. The sense of fear and abandonment is clear, yet hopeful trust emerges as the psalm continues:

> For he did not despise or abhor the affliction of the afflicted; he did not hide his face from me, but heard when I cried to him. (Ps 22:24)

Some might find it easy to imagine the great and holy God turning away as Jesus bears the sin of the world. After all, isn't sin abhorrent to God? Doesn't God *have* to wait until Jesus dies until he can turn his eyes back to the One called God's Son? Based on God's justice and holiness, doesn't God *have* to forsake Jesus?

"My God, my God, why have you forsaken me?" But these are the words of the praying community. They come from the sacred texts of prayer. They are spoken at the hour when the community prays. They are, perhaps, not words of *abandonment*, but words of *identification*.

When Jesus cries out with the prayers of his brothers and sisters, he identifies himself with *their* pain, *their* anguish, *their* fear that maybe God has left them to the whims of a world that seeks to devour them. For those who loved Jesus, their hopes and dreams had gone to the cross with him. When Jesus cried out in apparent forsakenness, those within hearing could identify with him, because he was identifying with them.

When we see Jesus on that cross, we are not observing an innocent third party— one who stands opposite God and the human race. Instead, in Jesus we see God on that cross, taking upon himself all the pain and suffering that the powers of evil can deliver. When Jesus speaks the prayer of the psalmist, we hear the very voice of God identifying with the anguish of all people, taking into himself the human inevitability of sin and death.

And when God takes that on, the power of sin and death is broken. Yes, sin and death still come. Sin and death are still part of the reality of human existence. But they will no longer have the last word. There is a new last word for us, and it comes in the closing words of the prayer that Jesus has borrowed from the psalmist:

> All the ends of the earth shall remember and turn to the LORD; and all the families of the nations shall worship before him. For dominion belongs to the LORD, and he rules over the nations. To him, indeed, shall all who sleep in the earth bow down; before him shall bow all who go down to the dust, and I shall live for him. Posterity will serve him; future generations will be told about the Lord, and proclaim his deliverance to a people yet unborn, saying that he has done it. (Ps 22:27–31)

"My God, my God, why have you forsaken me?" For Jesus, these were among his last words on the cross. For us, they become *first* words. We speak them first because in our pain and suffering, in our darkest moments of isolation and fear, we often wonder where God has gone. But these first words are only the preparation for the hope that is to come. When God has fully identified himself with us in the person of Jesus, we have no need to fear. We are never forsaken. These last words of Jesus catapult us into hopeful trust in the God who has done for us what we could never do for ourselves.

∽

In this homily I attempted to draw the listeners into the experience described in the text and to become hearers of Jesus' last words along with those who were witnessing his death and also translating the meaning of his words for them. It was also my hope to challenge the commonly-held idea that, on the cross, Jesus' words were cried out in despair because God—his heavenly Father, whom Jesus served with faultless obedience—had turned his back on his appointed sin-bearer. By linking Jesus' words with the Psalm from which they had been taken and to the fixed hours of Israel's communal prayer time, I wanted to move our thinking from God's assumed act of abandonment to his full identification with the people he loved.

WE HAVE SEEN THE LORD (JOHN 20:19–31)

The following sermon was preached on April 11, 2010 at a new and relatively small church where I had been invited to speak.

∼

> When it was evening on that day, the first day of the week, and the doors of the house where the disciples had met were locked for fear of the Jews, Jesus came and stood among them and said, "Peace be with you." After he said this, he showed them his hands and his side. Then the disciples rejoiced when they saw the Lord. Jesus said to them again, "Peace be with you. As the Father has sent me, so I send you." When he had said this, he breathed on them and said to them, "Receive the Holy Spirit. If you forgive the sins of any, they are forgiven them; if you retain the sins of any, they are retained."
> But Thomas (who was called the Twin), one of the twelve, was not with them when Jesus came. So the other disciples told him, "We have seen the Lord." But he said to them, "Unless I see the mark of the nails in his hands, and put my finger in the mark of the nails and my hand in his side, I will not believe." A week later his disciples were again in the house, and Thomas was with them. Although the doors were shut, Jesus came and stood among them and said, "Peace be with you." Then he said to Thomas, "Put your finger here and see my hands. Reach out your hand and put it in my side. Do not doubt but believe." Thomas answered him, "My Lord and my God!" Jesus said to him, "Have you believed because you have seen me? Blessed are those who have not seen and yet have come to believe." Now Jesus did many other signs in the presence of his disciples, which are not written in this book. But these are written so that you may come to believe that Jesus is the Messiah, the Son of God, and that through believing you may have life in his name. (John 20:19–31)

It is common for people to look for reasons why people have bad things happen to them. Death, outside of what is expected at old age, is something that often disturbs us at a very deep level, and we often look for reasons to explain why the death has taken place.

If I hear about a man my age, in reasonably good health, who falls over dead one day, I want some reasons. I want to know that he secretly smoked like a chimney, sat in front of the TV all day and ate Cheetos and Twinkies, and was a closet heroin addict. I need to know that there are any number of reasons why his brand of death won't be visited on me. I also want to believe that, somehow, death is not merely random.

Ever since the assassination of John F. Kennedy, people have been looking for reasons to explain high-profile deaths that go beyond the obvious. It isn't enough that the various commissions have determined that Kennedy was killed by a lone assassin; conspiracy theories still abound, implicating the Mafia, Kennedy's political opponents, the Vatican, or some dark, malevolent forces.

When Princess Diana died, conspiracy theories emerged as well, projecting murderous intentions on her boyfriend's questionable business associates and suggesting an evil plan generated by the Royal family. It just wasn't enough to recognize that when you ride in a car that is going far too fast for safety, and driven by an intoxicated driver, that you might actually get killed. People want other, more complex reasons for death.

Christians have been thinking about the death of Jesus for a very long time. In looking back on the Gospel accounts and the emergence of the early church, people have tried to get their minds around the significance of his death. Theories have abounded for centuries:

- Satan was holding the world ransom. God bargained with Satan by offering Jesus in exchange for the release of the world. Satan agreed, thinking he had the goods on God now, and then set about to kill Jesus. But when Jesus was raised from the dead, the deal was off and Satan knew he had been tricked.

- God is like a medieval lord or baron. When a peasant offends the baron, a price must be paid so that the baron's honor is restored. People have offended God through sin, and now a price must be paid, and the price is death. Since people are evil, their death doesn't count for anything, so the death of a true innocent is required. Jesus, the Son of God, is the only choice.

- The death of Jesus really only shows us the importance of obedience and sacrifice so that we would be influenced by Jesus' moral behavior.

- God has a need to punish human beings for their sin, and the punishment is death. That is how God's justice is restored. Jesus stands in our place—he is our substitute—suffering the penalty that should be ours so that we can be made right with God.

These theories of the atonement (how Jesus reconciles us to God) have been around for a long time—the last one being the more dominant among evangelical Christians today. People have tended to camp on one of these theories, setting the entire basis for Christian faith on them. There is a tendency to look at the death of Jesus through the various theological lenses that have been developed over the ages. But there are two things that might be helpful for us to remember:

1. The obvious answer to "Why did Jesus die?" is, He died because some people killed him.

2. Basing our Christian faith only on Jesus' death suggests that his resurrection might have been unnecessary.

First, the most obvious answer to the *why* question is that Jesus died because the Jewish religious leaders and the Romans conspired together to get rid of him. This is what happened to people who threatened the religious and political status quo (it still happens today). Jesus himself anticipated this, as quoted in Matthew 23:

> "Jerusalem, Jerusalem, the city that kills the prophets and stones those who are sent to it! How often have I desired to gather your children together as a hen gathers her brood under her wings, and you were not willing!" (Matt 23:37)

In another sense, we could say that Jesus died as a result of being born. If you think about it, this is pretty obvious. Every human being that is born gets a ticket to a funeral. That's how it works with us. If we really believe that the fullness of God was in Jesus, then when Jesus was conceived and then born, God—through Jesus—would ultimately experience human death. God would take death into himself and destroy its power, no matter the means of that death. God was not rolling the dice with Jesus, hoping that things would turn out. God fully identified himself with us from the start.

Second, when we look at the death of Jesus as though it is a kind of transaction that we claim for ourselves, which removes our sin and qualifies us for heaven, we risk marginalizing Jesus' resurrection. If the death of Jesus on the cross is all that we need, then resurrection is just a bonus. We celebrate it because it puts a happy ending on a very tragic story. We might even call it unnecessary. But we don't make that claim, do we? We claim that in the resurrection, sin and death are defeated, and we have the promise of resurrection for ourselves. It isn't the death of Jesus that defeats sin and death. At first glance, sin and death win when Jesus dies. It is the resurrection that destroys those powers.

In the text we read from John 20, Jesus comes to his disciples, still bearing the marks of his crucifixion. There is no theological explanation for his death offered to us, but instead the focus is on the fact that Jesus is alive. The marks on his body give the evidence of his death—people don't usually survive crucifixion, stabbing, and entombment. Thomas does all of us a big favor by doubting what he hasn't yet seen. I am blessed by Jesus' willingness to come back a week later to meet Thomas at his place of doubt. After seeing Jesus for himself, Thomas offers one of the most theologically rich statements about Jesus found in the Bible: "My Lord and my God!"

It is very interesting to me that Jesus doesn't focus so much on what just happened to him in terms of his death and resurrection, but rather on what is about to happen. He breathes on them, granting them the Holy Spirit. Then he sends them out, in the same way that God the Father has sent Jesus. There is no discussion about what has been accomplished by Jesus' death; there is only the new reality of the resurrection, and the commission for his disciples to participate in Jesus' work for the sake of the world.

In Revelation 21 Jesus declares that he was dead and is now alive forever and ever. He then states that he holds the keys of Death and Hades (Hades is not Hell as in popular imagery, but rather just the place where the dead go). John speaks dramatically about this part of his vision:

> When I saw him, I fell at his feet as though dead. But he placed his right hand on me, saying, "Do not be afraid; I am the first and the last, and the living one. I was dead, and see, I am alive for ever and ever; and I have the keys of Death and of Hades." (Rev 1:17–18)

The death and resurrection of Jesus are woven together in a very important way: In Jesus' death, God—the One who has fully identified himself with us—lets all the powers of evil have their way with him. Yes, Jesus dies in the sense that all people must die, but he dies at the hands of the powers that seek to replace God. When Jesus is raised from the dead, those powers are defeated. Sin and death are exposed for the imposters that they are—they have no rights over the ultimate destiny of the people God loves.

Jesus' death is important to us—and to the world—but perhaps in a larger way than we've imagined. In this Easter season we reflect on and celebrate all that has happened in Jesus. And, like his first followers, we are reminded that the risen Jesus has also breathed upon us. His Spirit has been granted to us, that we might join in on his ongoing ministry in the world.

I've noticed that when we focus on the death of Jesus as the single most important thing that God has done, we tend to focus on wrath, whether we see wrath as God's punishment for sin or as the way we suffer the consequences of trying to live life without God. Either way, we can end up seeing the death of Jesus on the cross as the way that wrath is derailed and we get to go to heaven when we die.

But there is a much larger picture for us to grasp. The work of God in Jesus is the pinnacle of what God has always been doing in the world—bringing reconciliation. Israel came into being as part of God's work to reconcile the world to himself. In Jesus, that work is reborn and relaunched through the power of the Holy Spirit.

The larger picture of reconciliation includes the death of Jesus, but is not limited to that death.

- In Jesus, God takes on human existence as a real person born into the real world.

- As a real person, Jesus lives, grows, relates, works, suffers, and dies and all humans will do.

- In the death of Jesus, God allows all the powers of evil—the powers that claim ultimate dominion in the world—to have their way with him. It is the violent act of destruction that seeks to eradicate God and his people from the earth.

- In the resurrection, God defeats those powers, destroying their claim over humanity. In Jesus' new life, a new Israel is born—an Israel that is no longer limited to the Jewish family, but now includes all who put their trust in Jesus. By the power of the Holy Spirit, these new people are sent into the world to proclaim and demonstrate the reality of the kingdom of God.

At the Margins of Ground Zero: Preaching the Atonement

It's a really big story. It's a story that is grounded, not in wrath, but in love. God does not do all that he does because he needs anger management. He does what he does out of his great love for all the creation, including us. And that love cuts God deeply, because love hurts.

Just this week my grandson, Jacob, suffered a seizure and had to be taken to the hospital. Jacob is diabetic, and while seizures are not entirely uncommon for diabetics, this was a first for him. The doctors sent him home without too much concern on their parts, and we were grateful for their calm responses. Jacob, because he's a strong kid and has to deal with a lot of health issues, just shrugged off the event and went off to play football and ride his bike, while the rest of us nursed the pain we experienced through Jacob's frightening event. Our shared pain was grounded in our deep love for him rather than in anything else. We would not have experienced such pain if it had not been preceded by love.

Out of love, God takes into himself all that is human, and bears the pain of suffering and death that is poured out by the very people he loves. The pain that God bears is a pain born of his love. Out of love, God crushes the power of sin and death, and sends his new, Spirit-breathed people to invite the world into the life of God. For their faithfulness, some of those people might also suffer and die. But death no longer retains its power to claim that the story is over.

Many of us here today have been around the church long enough to recognize that a lot of people see themselves as dodging the bullet of God's wrath by believing in Jesus. I've heard people say things that reveal their belief that God would really prefer to destroy all of us humans because of our filthy, rotten behavior, but he stops himself from doing that by sacrificing Jesus. He'd still like to do us in, but now Jesus runs interference and keeps that from happening. Some of you might find that interpretation to be funny; but I'm betting that others here find it disturbingly familiar. If you listen carefully, you'll even hear that there are some worship songs we sing that reinforce this way of thinking.

I have some good news for us today: What God has done in and through Jesus Christ through his birth, his life, his suffering, his death, and his resurrection is not about God keeping himself from global genocide. This amazing story of Jesus is grounded in God's love for the world, for his people throughout the ages, and for us sitting here today. I can say with confidence that you do not find new life in Jesus because God grudgingly brought it about; you have that new life because God, in his incomprehensible love for us, gave all of himself to us in Jesus.

∼

I knew that the people of this church were passionate in their faith and energetic about serving the community in which they were planted. I also recognized that some of them were new to the faith while others, although veterans of Christian discipleship, translated the atonement in terms of penal substitution and often explained the Gospel to others by using that framework. It was my hope to help the people who had come to see themselves as second-class citizens of faith to embrace the good news that they are truly the beloved of the God who has given his all to them in Jesus.

∼

The following are four pre-Easter messages delivered at Soulfarers Community, the church where I served as pastor, on April 9, 2000, March 24, 2002, April 13, 2003, and March 20, 2005, respectively.

∼

THE CONVICTION AND SENTENCING OF JESUS
(John 18:28—19:16)

What do we think of when we think of Jesus? This time of year we have a number of important images:

- Jesus is the one in the dirty purple robe; a crown of thorns on his head

- He is the one nailed to the horrible wooden cross—what the Greeks called the *staurós*.

- He is the one restored and risen, covered with resurrection light

But the Jesus we will see today is a man in custody. Jesus is a criminal. He has been cuffed and hauled off to jail. If he had any rights at all they would have been read to him by now.

Jesus spent three years preaching to people about the love of God and teaching them to live rightly before God. He expressed God's mercy and compassion by bringing healing and deliverance. He cleansed people's lives by forgiving their sins.

At the Margins of Ground Zero: Preaching the Atonement

Now he stands accused by his own people. He is humiliated and abused by the governmental authorities. He is rapidly becoming the victim of political and religious expediency.

The Jewish leaders and the Roman authorities intended to redirect Jesus' destiny. They intended to make an example of him and cut him out of their lives like a cancerous tumor. His destiny would be as an exile condemned to obscurity. He would soon be gone and forgotten. Or so they thought…

Please turn in your Bibles to John 18:28–40.

> Then the Jews led Jesus from Caiaphas to the palace of the Roman governor. By now it was early morning, and to avoid ceremonial uncleanness the Jews did not enter the palace; they wanted to be able to eat the Passover. So Pilate came out to them and asked, "What charges are you bringing against this man?" "If he were not a criminal," they replied, "we would not have handed him over to you." Pilate said, "Take him yourselves and judge him by your own law." "But we have no right to execute anyone," the Jews objected. This happened so that the words Jesus had spoken indicating the kind of death he was going to die would be fulfilled. Pilate then went back inside the palace, summoned Jesus and asked him, "Are you the king of the Jews?" "Is that your own idea," Jesus asked, "or did others talk to you about me?" "Am I a Jew?" Pilate replied. "It was your people and your chief priests who handed you over to me. What is it you have done?" Jesus said, "My kingdom is not of this world. If it were, my servants would fight to prevent my arrest by the Jews. But now my kingdom is from another place." "You are a king, then!" said Pilate. Jesus answered, "You are right in saying I am a king. In fact, for this reason I was born, and for this I came into the world, to testify to the truth. Everyone on the side of truth listens to me." "What is truth?" Pilate asked. With this he went out again to the Jews and said, "I find no basis for a charge against him. But it is your custom for me to release to you one prisoner at the time of the Passover. Do you want me to release 'the king of the Jews'?" They shouted back, "No, not him! Give us Barabbas!" Now Barabbas had taken part in a rebellion. (John 18:28–40, NIV)

Jesus spent the late evening hours on the Mount of Olives. He agonized in prayer; his disciples fell asleep, exhausted from the fear and sorrow that drained their energy. The temple officials and some soldiers arrived, led by Jesus' former follower—Judas Iscariot. The betrayal took its effect and Jesus was in the hands of his accusers.

The officials asked which one of the group was Jesus. When he identified himself they recoiled away from him and actually fell down all over each other. Were they shocked that he would be so bold as to step forward so quickly and submit himself to them? It doesn't seem they would be unraveled by something like that. Was it because when they asked for Jesus he responded by saying, "I am he"—a direct quote from Exodus 3:14, when God identified himself to Moses as the great I AM?

Jesus was taken to the high priest and questioned. When they didn't like his answers one of the officials hit Jesus in the face. It was a very safe thing to do. After all, Jesus' hands were tied. He was an easy target. It was also a very illegal thing to do. Jewish law did not allow someone—let alone an official of the high priest—to strike a person held captive.

Surely Jesus reacted physically when he was hit. He would be thrown off balance even more severely without the freedom of his hands to stabilize him. When he recovered from the blow he responded by saying,

> "If I said something wrong, testify as to what is wrong. But if I spoke the truth, why did you strike me?" (John 18:23)

According to John, Jesus received no answer.

Once the Jewish authorities finished with Jesus they dragged him to the local Roman governor, Pontius Pilate. It was the governor's practice to begin his day early and to receive important visitors at his palace. The representatives of the Jewish high priest would have been considered worthy of an immediate hearing—they didn't need an appointment.

Of course, the Jewish officials were very careful not to dirty their hands by violating their own ethics of purity. They had no intention of entering the dwelling place of a gentile ruler, thereby making themselves ceremonially unclean. At the same time they needed Pilate to accomplish their purposes. Having to come outside to accommodate these people must have been an irritation to Pilate.

They presented Jesus to Pilate as a criminal. For Pilate this label had no meaning coming from the Jews. They differed as to the definition of the word "crime." He recommended they settle whatever problem they had in their own little religious court.

But the Jews threw down a disturbing challenge to the Roman governor. This Jesus was a man worthy of execution. Executing their own people was not an act these Jews did easily. Something was very wrong here.

Evidently these Jews were not looking for justice—they were looking for extermination. Pilate knew that the Jews did not love the Romans. It appears Rome was now to be a useful tool to them. From the standpoint of the Jewish officials, a public crucifixion would seal the curse on Jesus by forever labeling him as an *unclean* criminal—one from whom even God himself would turn away. And if the Romans did the work of murder, then the Jewish leaders could keep their hands clean. After all, their distance from uncleanness was a high priority.

Pilate went back inside his palace. He had Jesus brought in so he could interrogate him privately. The Jewish leaders' obsession with ritual purity would guarantee that he could talk privately with this desperate man without the constant interruptions from the others.

As he questioned Jesus he knew this was no king. If the Jews had any kind of king it was that idiot Herod. This Jesus was just another crazy street preacher—obviously harmless but apparently a big problem for the Jews. *Pilate just didn't get it.*

Yet Pilate played along. When he directly asked Jesus the true nature of his crime, Jesus claimed,

> "My kingdom is not of this world. If it were, my servants would fight to prevent my arrest by the Jews. But now my kingdom is from another place." (John 18:36 NIV)

Now Pilate had to be sure that Jesus was deluded. Pilate knew the identities of any provincial leaders that were worth knowing. Jesus was not one of them. The strange nature of Jesus' answers to Pilate's questions suggested that Jesus was probably a philosophical teacher—there were certainly a lot of them wandering around.

So Jesus thought he was a king. He seemed to have a strange sense of his own destiny, because his only elaboration on his claim to be a king was to say,

> "For this reason I was born, and for this I came into the world, to testify to the truth. Everyone who belongs to the truth listens to my voice." (John 18:37)

Truth. What did truth mean to Pilate? What did it mean to anyone? If you listened to the Greek philosophers truth was impossible to fully grasp. Plato thought truth was found only in some unearthly dimension where all things are seen clearly. Aristotle agreed, and felt that nothing people saw or touched with their hands was truly real—certainly none of it was of any ultimate importance.

So when Pilate responded to Jesus by asking, "What is truth?" he wasn't looking for any answers. The question carried the assumption that there was no answer to be had. And Jesus gave him no response.

For Pilate, the Jews must have been the strangest people on earth. They got so worked up about things that just didn't matter to him. They wanted to execute this pathetic man, yet his only crime seemed to be having *ideas*. His only weapons were *words*.

Maybe the only way to resolve this issue would be to call their bluff; use some of their own religious nonsense against them. He knew their own custom was to release a prisoner as an act of mercy during the Passover celebration. He would use that custom to show them how ridiculous this whole thing was. He would offer to release a real criminal: Barabbas—a street thug, a bandit, a rebel against authority. Then they would see how harmless Jesus was by contrast.

But the ploy completely backfired. The crowd began screaming for the release of Barabbas like he was some kind of folk hero. Pilate couldn't believe it. These people were crazy.

The only thing left to do now would be to abuse and humiliate Jesus so the crowd would pity him. Pilate's soldiers did the job for him—flogging Jesus until the skin and muscles were torn from his back, draping an old discarded purple cloak over his torn up shoulders, forcing a crown of thorny branches around his head. But even then the crowd was unmoved.

Look with me at John 19:6–16 as we come to the end of this nightmare:

> As soon as the chief priests and their officials saw him, they shouted, "Crucify! Crucify!" But Pilate answered, "You take him and crucify him. As for me, I find no basis for a charge against him." The Jews insisted, "We have a law, and according to that law he must die, because he claimed to be the Son of God." When Pilate heard this, he was even more afraid, and he went back inside the palace. "Where do you come from?" he asked Jesus, but Jesus gave him no answer. "Do you refuse to speak to me?" Pilate said. "Don't you realize I have power either to free you or to crucify you?" Jesus answered, "You would have no power over me if it were not given to you from above. Therefore the one who handed me over to you is guilty of a greater sin." From then on, Pilate tried to set Jesus free, but the Jews kept shouting, "If you let this man go, you are no friend of Caesar. Anyone who claims to be a king opposes

Caesar." When Pilate heard this, he brought Jesus out and sat down on the judge's seat at a place known as the Stone Pavement (which in Aramaic is Gabbatha). It was the day of Preparation of Passover Week, about the sixth hour. "Here is your king," Pilate said to the Jews. But they shouted, "Take him away! Take him away! Crucify him!" "Shall I crucify your king?" Pilate asked. "We have no king but Caesar," the chief priests answered. Finally Pilate handed him over to them to be crucified. So the soldiers took charge of Jesus. (John 19:6–16, NIV)

Pilate feared that Jesus might be one of the wandering teachers that were thought to posses the power and wisdom of the gods. Even his own accusers were taking Jesus' own claims to be God's Son seriously.

But the Jewish leaders were done with trying to get Pilate to act out of religious respect. They would trade their moral outrage for political expediency. If Rome wouldn't execute someone for his philosophy, then surely they would execute him for treason. So the Jews labeled Jesus as a competitor to Caesar.

In an earlier exchange with Jesus the Jewish leaders let him know where their loyalties and passions were grounded. They told him,

"The only Father we have is God himself." (John 8:41, NIV)

Now their tune has changed. Their loyalties have shifted because their personal agendas must be fulfilled. They sealed Jesus' fate by guaranteeing to Pilate,

"We have no king but Caesar." (John 19:15b, NIV)

So now Jesus is on his way to his death. Of course, like all of us, he was on his way to death from the moment of his birth. But this death at the hands of his own people, this death that he embraced voluntarily, this death that became so public and so horrible would not be the defeat the Jewish leaders planned on. It would not be the quick solution that the Romans thought would quiet a minor controversy. *It was the death that showed God's initiative in love to a world that would just as easily kill him if they could.*

For Pilate, the only truth was political expediency. For Jesus, it was not time to debate about the truth, but to walk it out. Unlike Pilate, Jesus would not define truth as a view about the world and how it works. *Truth was the character and integrity of God's promise to redeem people from eternal destruction.*

Eventually the Jews succeeded in putting Jesus in his place. Their appeal to Roman authority took them, their arguments, and their perception of Jesus and packaged them up under the rule of Caesar. They would legitimize their own actions and minimize the impact of Jesus by placing them underneath the king of the civilized world. Then they could keep their hands clean.

The horrible machine is now in operation. This man called Jesus will be sentenced to an execution at the orchestration of his own people, a brutal brand of killing that even the Romans years later would outlaw because of its brutality. According to his accusers he was guilty of bringing in a new kingdom and claiming to have such an intimate relationship with God that he could call himself the Son of God. If they only knew how right they were.

Both the Roman and Jewish authorities wanted Jesus properly labeled and categorized so he could take his place of obscurity behind all the other really important things in the world. Having encountered Jesus they didn't want to get their hands dirty because of him. They wanted someone else to get involved with disposing of Jesus. Too much involvement on their part might lead to actually being affected by him.

2,000 years later as we think about these dramatic events leading to Easter we find ourselves in the place of getting our hands dirty by involvement with Jesus. Sometimes we place our perception of Jesus and our own walk of faith alongside everything else in our life—under the very rule of our culture. Jesus is okay with us—just as long as he and the community of Christians fit into the right timeslots of life.

Is Jesus just another "truth" along with the other "truths" of our lives? Do we put the truth of Jesus alongside

- The truth of our recreational and leisure needs?
- The truth of our careers and interests?
- The truth of our ambitions?

Jesus said,

> "For this I was born, and for this I came into the world, to testify to the truth. Everyone who belongs to the truth listens to my voice." (John 18:37b)

The only unshakable truth to be known is that God has come to us in Jesus to rescue us from meaninglessness, hopelessness and eternal separation from him.

It was not the Jewish and Roman rulers' actions that were important in the death of Jesus, but the initiative of God in bringing us a way to be restored to him and to enter a life that's worth living.

When God came to us in Jesus his hands got very dirty by his association with us. The apostle Paul summarized it for us this way:

> God demonstrates his own love for us in this: While we were still sinners, Christ died for us. (Romans 5:8, NIV)

What is the call for us today? It is to take Jesus out of the category of the convenient, the mundane, even the respectable and let his rule and kingdom take over our lives. Our lives will be ruled by something—culture, distraction, self-interest, the demands of other people. None of those kingdoms are worth living in. God has brought his kingdom to us in Jesus. There is no other worthy king beside him.

∽

In this message I attempted to bring people into the story of Jesus being marginalized, to the point of death, by those who found his message and actions to be contrary to the power-stories of the dominant cultures, both Jewish and Roman. In doing that I hoped that the people would come to grips with our own contemporary ways of marginalizing Jesus and paying tribute instead to the siren songs of our culture.

"SURELY NOT I, LORD!"

(Matt 26:20–28)

Today is Palm Sunday. Palm Sunday is the beginning of Holy Week and signals the last week of Lent. It calls us to stop and reflect on the great welcome given to Jesus as he entered into Jerusalem—right into the political expectations of the people who assumed Jesus had come to turn the Romans upside down. It was a dramatic example of human beings wanting God only on their own terms.

Those kinds of expectations continued to form the thinking of even Jesus' closest disciples. As the time of his death drew near his disciples found their expectations being taken down. He had spoken to them of his leaving, but now he spoke of betrayal and desertion:

> When it was evening, he took his place with the twelve; and while they were eating, he said, "Truly I tell you, one of you will betray me." And they became greatly distressed and began to say to him one after another, "Surely not I, Lord?" He answered, "The one who has dipped his hand into the bowl with me will betray me. The Son of Man goes as it is written of him, but woe to that one by whom the Son of Man is betrayed! It would have been better for that one not to have been born." Judas, who betrayed him, said, "Surely not I, Rabbi?" He replied, "You have said so." While they were eating, Jesus took a loaf of bread, and after blessing it he broke it, gave it to the disciples, and said, "Take, eat; this is my body." Then he took a cup, and after giving thanks he gave it to them, saying, "Drink from it, all of you; for this is my blood of the covenant, which is poured out for many for the forgiveness of sins." (Matt 26:20–28)

When Jesus announced that betrayal was in the air, each of his disciples took his turn to object: "Sure not I, Lord?" Jesus gives a little hint: It will be one who has shared food with him that night. Of course, that doesn't really help—everyone in the room has been sharing food. So the anxiety increases.

Judas, who knows exactly who Jesus is talking about, fakes his own protest: "Surely not I, Rabbi?" The others have addressed Jesus as Lord; only Judas begins to distance himself from Jesus by calling him *teacher*, or *rabbi*. Jesus' only response is to simply confirm Judas' word: "You have said so."

I like how this conversation is relayed in *The Message*:

> Then Judas, already turned traitor, said, "It isn't me, is it, Rabbi?" Jesus said, "Don't play games with me, Judas." (Matt 26:25, *The Message*)

In a way it seems that the others are off the hook, but their own failure is also just waiting to happen. Jesus tells them later,

> "You will all become deserters because of me this night; for it is written, 'I will strike the shepherd, and the sheep of the flock will be scattered.'" (Matt 26:31)

In the midst of this heart-breaking news Jesus introduces an act of remembrance that Christians have been participating in for 2,000 years: The Lord's Supper. He holds up the bread, using it to represent his body which is about to be nailed to a cross. Then he lifts a cup of wine, comparing it to his blood which will spill out during his time of abuse and suffering.

At the Margins of Ground Zero: Preaching the Atonement

But the comparison goes further: Jesus says his blood has something to do with *covenant*. It's like the ancient animal sacrifices that became the sealing of an agreement between parties. The sacrificial system that characterized ancient Judaism sealed the ancient covenant that God created: *I will be your God, and you will be my people*. In the coming death of Jesus, a covenant would be re-established—a covenant with God.

We who call ourselves Christians believe that God has made himself known to us in Jesus; that the man Jesus was truly God in the flesh. So the death of Jesus on the cross was so much more than just another good man losing his life for the benefit of others. It was God himself taking human death into himself in the death of Jesus.

What happens when the God of creation—the God who gives life—embraces human death into himself? What happens when God, the author of life, the one who creates all things out of nothing, the one who has no beginning and no end takes on human death into himself?

The Bible tells us,

> In the beginning God created the heavens and the earth. Now the earth was formless and empty, darkness was over the surface of the deep, and the Spirit of God was hovering over the waters. And God said…(Gen 1:1–3a, NIV)

When we speak of God creating something out of nothing we have to remember that nothing is not something. Nothing is not like anti-Play-Doh and God makes everything out of it. What precedes creation is the word of God—*And God said*…God speaks and there is creation; there is life.

Jesus on the cross is, in a very important sense, God on the cross. As the Gospel writer John says,

> In the beginning was the Word, and the Word was with God, and the Word was God. He was with God in the beginning. Through him all things were made; without him nothing was made that has been made. In him was life, and that life was the light of all people. The light shines in the darkness, but the darkness has not understood it. (John 1:1–5, TNIV)

Throughout the Bible God's covenant relationship with people comes from his initiative and his power. God's word—the word he speaks—precedes all of creation. When Jesus—God's word made flesh—went to the cross he took our death back to the place that comes before all of creation: To God's presence. Our lives now rest in his protective, healing grace.

Why is this important? Because like Jesus' first disciples, we sit around him saying, "Surely not I, Lord." We ask the question because we have this sneaking suspicion that all the wrong things we've done in our lives are equivalent to the nails that put Jesus on the cross. So we indirectly become the ones responsible for killing Jesus.

Don't you imagine that his disciples later felt some of that? Didn't they feel that if only there was no betrayal, if only they hadn't deserted him, then everything would have just turned out okay?

And we think: If only we wouldn't have failed so many times; if only we didn't have the life we've had, then Jesus wouldn't have to have died.

But we don't have that kind of power and no human ever has—not even the Romans. Jesus went to his death willingly. His death sealed God's covenant relationship with us. God's covenant comes by his initiative—not ours. It comes by his power—not ours.

Can you imagine the nails that were pounded through Jesus' body? Can you imagine him dying as a result of that agonizing experience on the cross?

Theologians have often spoken of Jesus' death as substitutionary: It was a substitute for our death. But that doesn't mean that his death happened *instead* of ours; we don't escape death. It means that he stepped into our place, and God, in Jesus, took death into himself.

But if his death was a substitute, then so was his suffering. The nails in Jesus' body not only inflicted pain but were also the devices for holding him in a painful place. Yes, Jesus died a human death—our death. But he also endured human suffering—our suffering.

And I have news for you: You didn't drive the nails into Jesus. These are *your* nails, taken from *your* life and heart and body and received into Jesus' body. He endured *our* suffering; he took on *our* death. Here's a great truth:

> But God demonstrates his own love for us in this: While we were still sinners, Christ died for us. (Romans 5:8, NIV)

Who are *the sinners*? Is it just a general term for everybody, since everybody has done bad things? Or is it more complex than that? In the Old Testament, forgiveness of sins included being released from exile; being allowed to return to the land of Israel after being taken captive by foreign invaders. In that company of exiles there were truly those who had been guilty of turning away from God. But there were also those who remained faithful to God who were swept up by war and defeat and captivity.

Think about the disciples for a moment:

- There was Judas: He had his own political agenda. He just didn't get was Jesus was about. While he surely had found a dark place of corruption in his life he was also duped by the religious leaders.
- There were the others: Yes, many did desert Jesus. Interestingly, the Greek word for *desert* also gives us the root for our word *scandal*. Along with meaning *to desert* it can also mean to *stumble*. The disciples stumbled not only in their own weakness but also in the face of a potentially violent attack. They were undoubtedly intimidated and overwhelmed by the mob that took Jesus away.

In the company of sinners are the ones who have sinned as well as the ones sinned against. And we all have nails in our bodies.

We have the nails that we have driven into ourselves because of our sin. Most of us can catalog a whole list of things we've done that we carry deep remorse over. Some of those things seem overwhelming and we can't imagine God ever getting over it. The pain of our regret seems never-ending.

We have the nails that others have driven into us. There has been abuse, abandonment, betrayal, dehumanization and brutality. We didn't put the nails there but we've had to organize our lives around them. And in the process we've driven more nails into ourselves and others.

Do you know the purpose of those nails in our lives? They are there for the purpose of defeat. They are there to keep us from hearing the voice of God. Each nail brings a message:

- *You aren't good for anything;*
- *You've done too much wrong to find forgiveness;*
- *God doesn't care about you;*
- *You just don't measure up;*
- *Your life is destined to be marked by regret.*

When Jesus goes to the cross he takes those nails with him; he takes them to the place of death. His message to us is that we no longer have to be defined by those nails and their dark messages. Yes, we may have to continue to deal and come to grips with the wounds and scars of those nails, but they no longer need to control, dominate and define us.

The nails also serve to bring accusation. Their presence in our lives confirms the failure we too often embrace as our identity.

When Jesus prepared his disciples for their coming roles as traitors and deserters, he wasn't bringing an accusation but was speaking a reality. And what do we find Jesus doing when he returns from the grave? He restores his disciples as his beloved friends.

When the nails are exposed in our lives it is easy for us to retreat into guilt and shame because we're pretty sure Jesus is shocked and angry with us. But the exposure of the sin we have done and the sin done to us is for the purpose of forgiveness and healing. That's what Jesus does when he gives his life: He takes those nails into his own body and carries them into his death. That is our only hope and it is the hope God has initiated in Jesus.

There is a table set before us today. On the table there is bread and wine. Those things represent for us the body and blood of Jesus. Often when we share in the Lord's Supper we come to remember and reflect on what he has done for us. But I believe today he wants us to take these things into our own bodies as we receive his substitutionary death in our own lives.

As you come to the table today you will see nails scattered all over it. When you take the bread and wine, take a nail—or, if you need to, take several—and drop them into the bowl. As you do this imagine that these nails are being taken from your life and given to Jesus, who will take them into his own body, taking them into his death. As you do this, release the sins you have done and the sins done to you. He will take them willingly, and will bring forgiveness and healing.

∽

In this message I looked at the atonement through the lens of substitution, but in a way that moved from the common penal theme to one that brought the possibility of liberation from the burden of regret that comes from sin. Rather than focus on sins committed by people that make them complicit in Jesus' death, I showed how at the cross Jesus takes on sin in its full spectrum—both the sins people have committed and those sins that have been inflicted by others. This opened the opportunity for both guilt and shame to be addressed in the lives of the people.

At the Margins of Ground Zero: Preaching the Atonement

THE STORY THAT IS BEING WRITTEN: PASSION
(John 21:27)

Here's a word that brings up some very interesting images: *Passion*. When you think of passion, maybe you see images of gothic romance novels. Or maybe you think of being passionately in love and being consumed by all the emotions and sensations that come with that experience.

When Emily and I became engaged, we were very much in love. All we could think about was our shared life that was about to come. We were consumed with thoughts and feelings toward one another. We were *passionate*. But I began to learn the true, deep meaning of passion when, only a few weeks after our engagement, I was shipped off to the other side of the country because I was in the U. S. Navy. Imagine my pain: Every waking moment was spent in the company of 75 other guys. We worked, marched, learned and took abuse together. Every night, the only sounds I heard were the sounds of 75 other young guys sleeping.

Yet, all my thoughts were with Emily. My passion for her now went beyond love. It went beyond desire. It truly became an experience of *suffering*.

When we think of passion we often think of romantic desire or deep devotion and enthusiasm for something. If we love cars then we say we have a *passion* for cars. If we love a certain kind of music then we say we have a *passion* for that music. Sometimes we even use that word in a spiritual way, saying that we desire to have a passion for God, or a passion for Jesus.

If we really understood the meaning of the word, we might not use it like we do.

In the ancient Greek language of the New Testament, *passion*—as it relates to sexual desire—is described by a word that suggests *the suffering of the mind*. I get that, don't you? That's why people deeply smitten by love often act so crazy. Even our English word *passion* comes from a Latin word that means *to suffer*. When we say we have com-passion, we are saying that we are entering into the suffering of another person.

Today is Palm Sunday—the Sunday before the celebration of Easter. We call it Palm Sunday because it commemorates the day that Jesus entered the city of Jerusalem, riding on a donkey, receiving the praise of the people. Yet, underlying the entire event is, for Jesus, a deep sense of sorrow and a preparation for his suffering and death yet to come. Today is also referred to as Passion Sunday, because it triggers the beginning of the horrible sufferings that Jesus would endure.

For many people, the events of this season bring up a number of questions: Why did Jesus have to die? Why is the cross so significant? What did all of this mean to the people back then, and what does it all mean to us now?

In order for us to begin to explore some of these questions, let's take a look at some very brief words of Jesus that will set the stage for us. These words come right after Jesus has used the analogy of the life cycle of a grain of wheat to predict not only his own pending death, but also the need for his followers to die to their old ways of life in order to experience the new life that God has for them.

Jesus said,

> "Now my soul is troubled. And what should I say—'Father, save me from this hour'? No, it is for this reason that I have come to this hour." (John 12:27)

There is so much packed into these few words. Jesus confesses that his soul is troubled. Imagine anticipating the kind of suffering and death Jesus was about to undergo. Surely he would be experiencing a sense of passion about his own life over the next few days. Jesus even speaks out what any of us would be thinking: The option to bail out. "Father, save me from this hour!" But Jesus discards that option, not because he is simply courageous, but because he understood his own destiny.

Once again, when I speak of destiny, I am not referring to fate or determinism. I am speaking of the idea of fulfilling one's mission in life, or to live out what one was made for. I think that is what Jesus was talking about.

It can be disturbing for us, standing on this side of Jesus' death, to wonder why we speak of his suffering, his passion, as something that happened *for* us? For that matter, what was it about his death that caused his followers, just a short time later, to refer to Jesus' dying in a similar way?

There have been a number of attempts to answer this question. Some have suggested that God was angry with the world and needed a clean, innocent human death in order to appease his anger and make it possible for people to escape his wrath. There was an ancient theory that said Jesus died because Satan was holding the human race hostage. God gave Jesus over to death as a kind of ransom payment so that Satan would let the people go. Once that was done, God tricked Satan by raising Jesus from the dead, thereby cheating Satan. Satan has been raising hell ever since.

Those theories can really bog us down unless we continue to try to connect with the larger story that is being written. In order to do that today, let's reflect back on some events that took place long before the birth of Jesus.

The ancient people of Israel had been enslaved in Egypt. They had long since lost their sense of identity as God's people, as a people for him, for the sake of the world. The idea that they had been raised up to bless all the nations of the world was just a fuzzy memory.

The Bible says that God responded to their suffering. He was compassionate toward them. Through Moses he set the stage for their rescue from their Egyptian captors.

Each family was ordered to obtain a lamb that was without any kind of blemish. They were to kill the lamb and, before cooking it for a family meal, they were to put some of the fresh blood of that lamb on the doorposts of the house. During the night God would pass through the country and take the life of the first born of each house where that blood mark was not evident. Then the people would be prepared for what God was about to do: Rescue them from their exile, from their captivity.

For centuries the Jewish people had celebrated this rescue with an annual feast called Passover. They would share a highly symbolic meal together that would call them to remember how God had rescued them from their exile. Some of those celebrations became times of both sorrow and hope, because the people would again find themselves in exile—suffering the consequences of forgetting and turning away from God as a nation.

On the night he was betrayed and turned over to the authorities for his trial and ultimate execution, Jesus shared a meal with his friends. Strangely enough, he even shared that meal with Judas, who facilitated the betrayal. Many scholars believe that this was more than just a meal, but a Passover observance. It was clear that the food items had meaning for them. Jesus focuses on two: The bread and the wine.

The bread used in the original Passover meal in Egypt and in the subsequent observances was unleavened—that is, without yeast. For the ancient Hebrews, yeast was a symbol of sin. The significance of eating bread without yeast was that it represented the setting aside of the people for God's love and purposes. They would not be set aside for the consequences of sin; they would be set aside for God.

The wine that was used in the Passover meal symbolized the lamb's blood that was put on the doorposts of the homes in Egypt. It represented

Atonement at Ground Zero

God's care and protection, as well as the anticipation that the rescue from exile was about to take place.

Jesus brought new meaning to these ancient symbols. He claimed that the bread represented his body and the wine represented his blood. What could this mean? It seemed to mean that, through Jesus, God was about to bring a rescue from exile. This rescue would not be from the exile brought about by their Roman oppressors, but rather from the enslavement of the sin that kept them de-centered from God.

But why did Jesus *have* to die? Did he *have* to die because of us? No, he *had* to die because he was born. When Jesus was born, it was guaranteed that one day he would die, just like any human being.

There is something very important in coming to grips with this. If God became human in the person of Jesus, then it was a guarantee that he would experience human death. God would experience what all humans experience. The initiative that God took in Jesus was not a plan that might have failed. Through Jesus, God would break the power of sin and death over human beings. When Jesus was born, that was a done deal.

So, why then is the cross important? Is it important because it is the cross? No—it is the cross because it is important. Was God dependent upon the cross to accomplish his plan? What if Jesus had died while being beaten and scourged? Would God have been foiled? No. To say that would mean that the cross—that wooden device of torture and death—had, in a way, more power than God himself. The cross is not important simply because it is the cross.

The cross is important because Jesus' death happened that way.

Like many ancient Hebrew prophets, Jesus lived out his life in ways that spoke deeply and symbolically to the Jewish people. The things he did—clearing out the temple, healing people, redefining the elements of the Passover meal—all pointed to a new reality being introduced by God.

Jesus had been denouncing the Jewish people's reactions to their Roman captors. On the one hand, he denounced the Jewish leadership's use of the same kind of power games to control people. On the other hand, he also denounced their use of violence to try to overthrow their captors—that was to use Rome's own weapons. Instead, he called the people to the way of peace, the way of love—that was the way to God's true kingdom.

Jesus knew where this path would lead. The people did not listen. They did not turn their lives to God, centering themselves on him. So Jesus willingly went to the place that would be inevitable for the people—the cross. In his death, Jesus was taking upon himself the tragic destiny of the people. Israel's battle against her captors would be lost—and Jesus willingly became Israel's representative, losing the battle on her behalf.

Think about it: The Roman cross was the place for losers! Roman citizens who were sentenced to death were even spared the cross. They were usually beheaded. The cross was for slaves, criminals and rebels operating outside the scope of Rome's respectability. Even the Jewish people saw the cross as place cursed by God. It was a place for losers. Jesus became a loser for his people.

Yet, even in the anticipation of his death, Jesus saw what was coming. He would not simply be a martyr, suffering a public death so that his own countrymen would be safe while the rest of the world passed by. Something much bigger was going on. Jesus said,

> "Whoever believes in me believes not in me but in him who sent me. And whoever sees me sees him who sent me. I have come as light into the world, so that everyone who believes in me should not remain in the darkness." (John 12:44–46)

In these words Jesus shows that he comes as God's agent, God's representative to the people of Israel. At the same time, he comes to be Israel's representative—to be the light of the world. That was supposed to be Israel's destiny. Jesus would now take that destiny upon himself. But his work would not stop with his own people—it would extend out to the entire world.

I don't believe that Jesus was intending to create a kind of unreasonable spiritual exclusivity in these words. I don't think he was trying to say that all the people in China who died that day would slide tragically into Hell by virtue of living too far away to hear Jesus speak. But that's a topic for another day.

What might this have meant to the first Christians 2,000 years ago? It seemed to mean that, in Jesus, the ultimate consequence for Israel's separation from God was suffered. It meant that, in Jesus, God would bring a new rescue to Israel. That rescue would now look like becoming a new people—a people for God, for the sake of the world. The invitation to be that new people of God would now be extended to the whole world. All who would trust their lives to Jesus—trusting, in effect, in the God who had sent him—would become that new people; they would become the light of the world.

What does it really mean for us? All of the failure and sin of Israel are representative of the failure and sin of the entire world. They are representative of our failure and sin. When Jesus willingly went to his death—a cursed, horrible death on a cross—he became a loser on our behalf. He became a loser so that we wouldn't have to. He took on himself all the consequences of sin and bore them on that cross. And now we are called to live out our lives as God's people—a people for God, for the sake of the world; we are called to live as the light of the world.

Why did Jesus die? He willingly went to his execution because that was where we were going.

Why is the cross important? Because that's how it happened. And in the resurrection and the drama that follows that amazing event, we will see how our lives, through what God has done in and through Jesus Christ, draws us into God's mission in the world.

BREAKING THE ILLUSION

(Matthew 21:1-17)

Today is Palm Sunday. This is the Sunday that begins Holy Week in the church year, as we prepare for the great celebration of Easter. The season of Lent concludes this Saturday.

We call today Palm Sunday because on this day we recall Jesus coming into Jerusalem, being welcomed and celebrated by the crowds just one week before they watched him being nailed to a cross. Because palm branches factored into the welcoming of Jesus, we call it Palm Sunday.

Let's read together about this great entrance into Jerusalem in Matthew, 21:1-17:

> When they had come near Jerusalem and had reached Bethphage, at the Mount of Olives, Jesus sent two disciples, saying to them, "Go into the village ahead of you, and immediately you will find a donkey tied, and a colt with her; untie them and bring them to me. If anyone says anything to you, just say this, 'The Lord needs them.' And he will send them immediately." This took place to fulfill what had been spoken through the prophet, saying, "Tell the daughter of Zion, Look, your king is coming to you, humble, and mounted on a donkey, and on a colt, the foal of a donkey." The disciples went and did as Jesus had directed them; they brought the donkey and the colt, and put their cloaks on them, and he sat

on them. A very large crowd spread their cloaks on the road, and others cut branches from the trees and spread them on the road. The crowds that went ahead of him and that followed were shouting, "Hosanna to the Son of David! Blessed is the one who comes in the name of the Lord! Hosanna in the highest heaven!" When he entered Jerusalem, the whole city was in turmoil, asking, "Who is this?" The crowds were saying, "This is the prophet Jesus from Nazareth in Galilee." Then Jesus entered the temple and drove out all who were selling and buying in the temple, and he overturned the tables of the money changers and the seats of those who sold doves. He said to them, "It is written, 'My house shall be called a house of prayer'; but you are making it a den of robbers." The blind and the lame came to him in the temple, and he cured them. But when the chief priests and the scribes saw the amazing things that he did, and heard the children crying out in the temple, "Hosanna to the Son of David," they became angry and said to him, "Do you hear what these are saying?" Jesus said to them, "Yes; have you never read, 'Out of the mouths of infants and nursing babies you have prepared praise for yourself'?" He left them, went out of the city to Bethany, and spent the night there.

This is a story of people living in a false reality. This is a story of people whose expectations about God and their own place in the world were all part of a delusion.

There is a growing sense of anticipation as Jesus sends his followers out to get his transportation ready for his entrance into the city. Matthew's own commentary on this links this event to an Old Testament prophecy in the book of Zechariah: *Look, your king is coming to you…*

As Jesus rode into the city there must have been some very mixed responses. The Roman peacekeepers in the city may have initially been alarmed if they heard that someone being hailed as a king—a rival to Caesar—was storming the gates of Jerusalem. But when they saw Jesus—a simple, humble man—riding on a donkey, they would have shrugged him off as a local nut.

It would be different for the Jewish people. They were a people living in occupied territory, and had for generations. There was, for them, always the underlying hope that, one day, their Messiah would come. That Messiah would be chosen by God to liberate them and destroy their enemies. They expected him to be a descendant of king David, and as any triumphant king, the Messiah would reinstate the order of power and peace that they believed was their birthright.

So their expectations about Jesus would have been filled with great hope and anticipation. And those expectations would characterize their world of *false reality*.

What was that false reality? It was a view of life and God that dominated the culture:

- False Reality #1: *Centers of power bring peace.* In one way the power of Rome brought peace. All enemies had been conquered and the powerful hand of Rome kept life contained and ordered. Yet the Jewish people wanted Rome out, so that their own structures of power could be reinstated in the name of God. The entrance of Jesus into the city elevated the hopes of the people that there would be a power transfer and that things would now go their way.

- False Reality #2: *The rich are blessed; the poor are cursed.* This was a common belief among the Jewish people. Rich people were special—blessed by God. The evidence of that blessing was found in their possessions. To be poor was to live outside of God's material blessings. In their anticipation that the power structures would be overturned would be found the hope that the economic structures would also be overturned.

- False Reality #3: *The healthy are righteous; the sick are sinful.* In that time and culture a sick or physically afflicted person was seen as suffering some sort of consequence. For example, when Jesus encountered a man born blind, his disciples wanted to know if it was the man's sin or the sin of his parents that caused the problem.

- False Reality #4: *Death is something that is ultimately denied by the life of the nation.* In the history of Israel the long line of kings—many of which were corrupt—created a royal establishment that outlived everyone. In the ongoing life of the royal houses of Israel the reality of human death didn't seem so final. Sure, people would die, but the nation would live on and on. Maybe, with the coming of the Messiah, there would be no end to the great nation of Israel. Then the denial of death could continue.

This view of life and God had created a world of illusion for the people. And into that illusion Jesus rode on a donkey and began to tear apart the fabric of misperception—their false reality was about to be disrupted. And the truth they would see would be very disturbing.

At the Margins of Ground Zero: Preaching the Atonement

The people who welcomed Jesus into Jerusalem saw the truth about their domination by Rome, but they falsely believed that replacing that dominance with a dominance of their own making would solve all their problems. It would just end up being the trading of one form of dominance for another. Their own history throughout the centuries had already proven that.

They saw the coming Messiah as God's agent for restoring their illusion. They wanted more food, more security, more power, more identity, more freedom. None of those things were necessarily bad or destructive—but in and of themselves they were an illusion of ultimate meaning and purpose in life.

So Jesus' triumphant entrance into Jerusalem was not a triumph over political power. It was a triumph over the illusion *that there can be life without God*; or the illusion that life *with* God is characterized by *success* as defined by the dominant culture.

Jesus very rapidly began to dismantle the illusion of the people.

- He dismantled the illusion of economic power as the fruit of God's approval. Jesus entered the temple courts and overturned the tables of the exploiters of worship. They had fooled the poor into believing that only the goods purchased here were acceptable by God. Jesus jumped into the middle of that program and dropped a virus into it. That religious exploitation would never be the same.

- Jesus also ripped out the firewall that had been constructed between the sick, suffering people—the outcasts of respectable life—and the grace and mercy of God. Jesus reached his hand out to them and healed them—destroying the illusion that sickness and death were the appropriate destiny for God's forgotten children.

- Then he shattered their false expectations by leaving the city. Jerusalem was a power center. It was the right place for the Messiah to be. All eyes would be set on Jesus as he centered himself in his power right in the temple: *Jerusalem's motherboard*. Instead, after shredding the fabric of the great illusion, he turned and left the city.

In a few days the people would see the truth about Jesus—the one who truly had come from God to rescue the people—and that truth would horrify them. That truth would be thrust in their faces in the form of a cross, and the one they thought would turn over the seats of power would be nailed to that cross, preparing to die as an outcast and failure.

Every one of us today has the potential of operating in a world of illusion. There are realities to what we do: We have to work, we have to engage in interpersonal relationships, we have to operate in the world of technology, we have to deal with material, financial and political issues. Those things in themselves are not illusions. But the illusion is found in a world that says those things are where we find ultimate meaning; where we find worth and definition; where we find some worthy version of God.

There are certainly those who think there is life without God. For them, these illusions are all that exist. Jesus encountered that among the Romans, whose sense of God was so diluted by empty paganism and multiple deities that it made little sense for many people. He encountered a different kind of mindset among his Jewish countrymen—that to be favored by God equaled being favored within society.

We need to face off with our illusions. When we anticipate Jesus, what do we expect he will bring to us?

- Will it be a perfect marriage? Maybe a perfect life partner? A perfect family?
- Perhaps it will mean an end to all financial problems, or that promotion or even the new career that we've been dreaming of.
- How about just a general sense of success in life? Or a removal of all uncertainty—answers to all our questions? Or the removal of all pain?

All those things would be great. And when we trust Jesus with our lives we do find healing and restoration in so many ways. But the hard reality Jesus brings us is the confrontation of death—his death on our behalf, not so that we might enjoy prosperity, but so that we might know the life of God; and also our death for his sake: Death to the illusion that we can expect anything more than Jesus. To expect anything else is to remain a slave to those expectations.

As in our time, a number of people in Jesus' day thought they had found freedom, when in truth they had not.

> Then Jesus said to the Jews who had believed in him, "If you continue in my word, you are truly my disciples; and you will know the truth, and the truth will make you free." They answered him,

> "We are descendants of Abraham and have never been slaves to anyone. What do you mean by saying, 'You will be made free'?" Jesus answered them, "Very truly, I tell you, everyone who commits sin is a slave to sin. The slave does not have a permanent place in the household; the son has a place there forever. So if the Son makes you free, you will be free indeed." (John 8:31–36)

The truth for us today is that to know and trust Jesus is to know and trust him *first of all* in his death. Paradoxically, in that death we find life and freedom. Yes, we continue to go to work, pay our taxes, vote for leaders, invest money and work on our relationships. But there is no more illusion: When those things are stripped away from us, we remain confronted with the cross of Jesus.

There are so many things that have captured our full attention. While many of those things are just the things of life, they are destined to fade and crumble. In and of themselves they can bring no final meaning to us. By themselves, money, family, careers, and even answers to our big questions are temporary things. They are a transient reality where too many people have pinned their hopes. Yet, behind them all is the true reality that Jesus has died for us. In his death, died on our behalf, we find our lives. That finding is eternal, not temporary.

Conclusion

When I became a church-planting pastor in my mid-forties, I found myself confronted not only with the organizational and leadership issues endemic to that process, but also with how I communicated key issues of faith to the people who gathered together in worship with me. In those early days when I would touch on the significance of the death of Jesus, I felt as though I was bumping against a wall. I believed his death to be important—even crucial—to our faith, but there was something in the way I had always heard it preached that caused me to stop short. I kept wrestling with the idea that God the Father somehow needed for someone—anyone, for that matter—to die in order for people to be forgiven. For one thing, God graciously granted forgiveness for sins in the Old Testament without dispatching anyone as a substitute. Why now?

My seminary training gave me plenty of space to wrestle with this issue, but a key experience came in the winter of 2005 at a pastor's seminar at Fuller Theological Seminary. Twenty-five pastors gathered for a week to interact with some of Fuller's top scholars to explore what was offered in the seminar title: Contemporary Images of the Atonement. It was there that I was introduced to the first edition of Mark Baker and Joel Green's book, *Recovering the Scandal of the Cross*.

I was relieved to discover that other pastors were also struggling with the dominant theme of penal substitution. They were hungry to explore the deeper story of the atonement, and we joined together to do that. Since that time, the atonement as a key topic of Christian faith has remained bright and shimmering at my consciousness.

Bible translators appear to have been wrestling with the issue as well, as evidenced by the change of language in First John 4:10 that has taken place over the years. The traditional King James Version uses the word *propitiation*—the satisfying of God's wrath—to describe what God had done in sending Jesus to die for us. The 1973 Revised Standard Version preferred the word *expiation*, suggesting that in the death of Jesus something had changed in human beings to make them acceptable to God. More recent translations, such as the New Revised Standard Version or the New International Version now employ the term "atoning sacrifice," a term rich in imagery yet remaining open to interpretation.

I began this book by asking the questions, "Why *this* one? Does this death *mean* something?" I have tried to answer the first by claiming that Jesus died, not because God needed something for himself or that he needed for humans to be altered before he would accept them, but rather because in Jesus God has imprinted his own image and brought his fullness to live with all of us who are mortal (Col 1:13–22). Jesus' death means something, not as a cosmic transaction, but instead as the inevitable identification with the human race that God takes into himself in the person of Jesus.

Atonement is incarnational because it is about God and his initiating love toward all people. Atonement is eschatological because in the resurrection God's intended future is demonstrated in the particularity of human history. And atonement is missional because through all that God has done in and through Jesus, we are drawn into God's redeeming, reconciling work for the sake of the world.

Atonement is a big story, and it is our story. It is a story unlike any other, and the way it is proclaimed and demonstrated is not incidental to the life shared by Christian communities all over the world. The multifaceted imagery of the Bible when it comes to atonement should keep us from concretizing any one theory and free us to explore the rich and diverse nature that allows atonement to be preached in every land to all people who experience life and hope in unique ways.

Above all else, the expansiveness and wonder of what God has done for the human race in and through Jesus the Christ brings us to our knees in gratitude and praise, embracing the invitation given to us by one who speaks with that great cloud of witnesses, the communion of the saints:

> Let us therefore approach the throne of grace with boldness, so that we may receive mercy and find grace to help in time of need. (Heb 4:16)

Bibliography

Anderson, Gary A. *Sin: A History*. New Haven: Yale University Press, 2009.
Anderson, Ray S. *On Being Human: Essays in Theological Anthropology*. Pasadena: Fuller Seminary Press, 1982.
———. *The Gospel According to Judas: Is There a Limit to God's Forgiveness?* Colorado Springs: NavPress, 1994.
Aulén, Gustaf. *Christus Victor*. London: SPCK, 2010.
Baker, Mark D. *Proclaiming the Scandal of the Cross: Contemporary Images of the Atonement*. Grand Rapids: Baker Academic, 2006.
Baker, Mark D. and Joel B. Green. *Recovering the Scandal of the Cross*. Downers Grove, IL: InterVarsity Press, 2011.
Bauckham, Richard. *The Theology of the Book of Revelation*. New York: Cambridge University Press, 1993.
Bercot, David. *A Dictionary of Early Christian Beliefs*. Peabody, MA: Hendrickson Publishers, 1998.
Boersma, Hans. *Violence, Hospitality, and the Cross: Reappropriating the Atonement Tradition*. Grand Rapids: Baker Publishing, 2004.
Bonhoeffer, Dietrich. *Christ the Center*. San Francisco: HarperCollins, 1978.
Brueggemann, Walter. *Hopeful Imagination: Prophetic Voices in Exile*. Philadelphia: Fortress Press, 1986.
———. *The Prophetic Imagination*. Minneapolis: Fortress Press, 1978.
———. *The Word That Redescribes the World*. Minneapolis: Fortress Press, 2006.
Burge, G. M. "John, Letters of." In *Dictionary of the Later New Testament and Its Developments*, edited by Ralph P. Martin and Peter H. Davids, 595. Downers Grove: InterVaristy Press, 1997.
Capon, Robert Farrar. *The Foolishness of Preaching: Proclaiming the Gospel against the Wisdom of the World*. Grand Rapids: William B. Eerdmans, 1998.
Carroll, John T. and Joel B. Green. *The Death of Jesus in Early Christianity*. Peabody, MA: Hendrickson Publishers, 1995.
Childs, Brevard S. *Biblical Theology of the Old and New Testaments*. Minneapolis: Fortress Press, 1992.
Eusebius Pamphilius, *Church History*, book V, chapter 24.2. Online http://www.ccel.org/ccel/schaff/npnf201.iii.x.xxv.html.
Goldingay, John. *Old Testament Theology: Israel's Gospel*. Downer's Grove: InterVarsity Press, 2003.
Green, Joel B. "Death of Jesus." In *Dictionary of Jesus and the Gospels*, edited by Joel B. Green, et al, 153. Downers Grove: InterVarsity Press, 1992.
———, "Kaleidoscopic View." In *The Nature of the Atonement*, edited by James Beilby and Paul R. Eddy, 158. Downers Grove: InterVarsity Press, 2006.
Grenz, Stanley J. *Theology for the Community of God*. Grand Rapids, MI: Wm B. Eerdmans, 1994.
Hauerwas, Stanley. *Cross-Shattered Christ*. Grand Rapids: Brazos Press, 2004.
Helm, Paul et al, *God and Time: Four Views*. Downers Grove: IVP Academic, 2001.
Heschel, Abraham J. *The Prophets*. New York: HarperCollins, 2001.

Bibliography

Hurtado, L. W. "Gospel (Genre)," in *Dictionary of Jesus and the Gospels*, edited by Joel B. Green, Scot McKnight, I. Howard Marshall, 279. Downers Grove: InterVarsity Press, 1992.

James, M. R., translator. "The Gospel of Nicodemus, or The Acts of Pilate." VII. Online http://www.earlychristianwritings.com/text/gospelnicodemus.html.

Jensen, Robert W. "How Does Jesus Make a Difference?" In *Essentials of Christian Theology*, edited by William C. Placher, 204–5. Louisville: Westminster John Knox Press, 2003.

Kirk, J. R. Daniel. *Unlocking Romans: Resurrection and the Justification of God*. Grand Rapids: William B. Eerdmans, 2008.

Kraus, C. Norman. *Jesus Christ Our Lord*. Scottdale, PA: Herald Press, 1990.

Lawley, James and Penny Tompkins. *Metaphors in Mind: Transformation through Symbolic Modeling*. London: The Developing Company Press, 2003.

Long, Thomas G. *The Witness of Preaching*. Louisville: Westminster John Knox Press, 2005.

Marshall, I. Howard. *New Testament Theology*. Downers Grove: InterVarsity Press, 2004.

Mays, James L. *Psalms*. Louisville: Westminster John Knox Press, 1994.

McKnight, Scot. *A Community Called Atonement*. Nashville: Abingdon Press, 2007.

———. "McLaren Emerging," *Christianity Today*, October 26, 2011. Online http://www.christianitytoday.com/ct/article_print.html?id=59862.

———, *The King Jesus Gospel*. Grand Rapids: Zondervan, 2011.

McLaren, Brian D. *Everything Must Change: Jesus, Global Crises, and a Revolution of Hope*. Nashville: Thomas Nelson, 2007.

Michaels, J. Ramsey. *1 Peter*. Word Biblical Commentary. Waco, TX: Word Books, 1988.

Muers, Rachel. "Adoptionism." In *Heresies and How to Avoid Them: Why it matters what Christians believe*, edited by Ben Quash and Michael Ward, 54. Peabody MA: Hendrickson Publishers, 2007.

Nolland, John. *Luke 18:35—24:53*. Eds. Metzger, Bruce M., et al. Word Biblical Commentary. Dallas: Word Books, 1993.

Pagitt, Doug. *Preaching in the Inventive Age*. Minneapolis: Sparkhouse Press, 2011.

Pinnock, Clark. *The Openness of God: A Biblical Challenge to the Traditional Understanding of God*. Downers Grove: IVP Academic, 1994.

Placher, William C. *How Does Jesus Save?* Christian Century (June 2, 2009), 26.

Reilly, Wendell. "Joseph Caiphas." *The Catholic Encyclopedia*. Online <http://www.newadvent.org/cathen/03143b.htm>

Ryken, Leland et al, "Atonement," in *Dictionary of Biblical Imagery*. Downers Grove, IL: InterVarsity Press, 1998.

Sanders, John. *The God Who Risks: A Theology of Providence*. Downers Grove: InterVarsity Press, 1998.

Shirer, William L. *The Rise and Fall of the Third Reich*. New York: Simon and Schuster, 1960.

Stanton, Graham N. *The Gospels and Jesus*. New York: Oxford University Press, 1989.

Taylor, Barbara Brown. *The Preaching Life*. Cambridge, MA: Cowley Publications, 1993.

Tennent, Timothy C. *Theology in the Context of World Christianity*. Grand Rapids: Zondervan, 2007.

Thompson, Marianne Meye. *The God of the Gospel of John*. Grand Rapids: William B. Eerdmans, 2001.

Bibliography

Torrance, James B. *Worship, Community & The Triune God of Grace*. Downers Grove: InterVarsity Press, 1996.
Torrance, Thomas F. *The Mediation of Christ*. Colorado Springs: Helmers & Howard, 1992.
Walker, Michael. *Laurel Canyon: The Inside Story of Rock and Roll's Legendary Neighborhood*. New York: Faber and Faber, 2006.
Weaver, J. Denny. *The Nonviolent Atonement*. Grand Rapids: William B. Eerdmans Publishing, 2001.
Williams, D. J. "Judas Iscariot," in *Dictionary of Jesus and the Gospels*. Downers Grove: Intervarsity Press, 1992.
Wright, Christopher J. H. *The Mission of God*. Downers Grove: InterVarsity Press, 2006.
Wright, John W. *Telling God's Story: Narrative Preaching for Christian Formation*. Downers Grove: InterVarsity Press, 2007.
Wright, N. T. *Evil and the Justice of God*. Downers Grove: InterVarsity Press, 2006.
———. *Jesus and the Victory of God*. Minneapolis: Fortress Press, 1996.
———. *Surprised by Hope*. New York: HarperCollins, 2008.
———. *The Challenge of Easter*. Downers Grove: InterVarsity Press, 2009.
———. *The New Testament and the People of God*. Minneapolis: Fortress Press, 1992.
———. *What Saint Paul Really Said*. Grand Rapids: Eerdmans Publishing, 1997.
Wright, Scott. *Oscar Romero and the Communion of the Saints*. Maryknoll, NY: Orbis Books, 2009.

www.ingramcontent.com/pod-product-compliance
Lightning Source LLC
Chambersburg PA
CBHW050805160426
43192CB00010B/1653